We Are Here

Fiona Harari is an award-winning journalist, and the author of *A Tragedy in Two Acts: Marcus Einfeld and Teresa Brennan.*

Fiona Harari

We Are Here

Talking with Australia's oldest Holocaust survivors

SCRIBE
Melbourne • London

Scribe Publications
18–20 Edward St, Brunswick, Victoria 3056, Australia
2 John Street, Clerkenwell, London, WC1N 2ES, United Kingdom

First published by Scribe 2018

Typeset in Adobe Garamond Pro by the publishers

Printed and bound in Australia by Griffin Press

The paper this book is printed on is certified against the Forest Stewardship Council® Standards. Griffin Press holds FSC chain of custody certification SGS-COC-005088. FSC promotes environmentally responsible, socially beneficial and economically viable management of the world's forests.

9781925322651(paperback edition)
9781925548464 (e-book)

A CiP record for this title is available from the National Library of Australia.

scribepublications.com.au
scribepublications.co.uk

Tomorrow I must begin a new life. How could I do it, with nothing but death behind me?

Władysław Szpilman,
HOLOCAUST SURVIVOR AND AUTHOR OF *THE PIANIST*

Contents

Introduction

This is a book about time, its passage, and its stagnation, as much as its distortion. It is about a future that extended longer than anyone imagined, and a past that is always present.

Tens of millions of people died during World War II, more than in any other war in history. Among its victims were six million Jews. Their murders, by Nazi Germany and its collaborators, were part of a systematic plan, which came to be known as the Final Solution, to exterminate Jewish people.

By the time Germany surrendered in May 1945, two-thirds of European Jewry was dead. So were tens of thousands of Romani, Jehovah's Witnesses, and German male homosexuals, among the many who had been systematically brutalised under Adolf Hitler's regime.

For those who outlived Nazism's worst intentions, surviving did not of itself inspire joy. Across the continent, cities had been destroyed, homes demolished, communities displaced and all but eradicated. As Europe was slowly rebuilt, those liberated from its concentration and forced-labour camps, and from its hidden corners where they had cowered silently for seeming aeons, emerged to a depleted and dramatically different life. Unfed, unwashed, and often close to death, some still clothed in the flimsy striped uniforms that marked them as concentration-camp prisoners, many were the sole survivors of once vast families. Now, having been deprived of a normal life for years, their education often stunted, they had to resume living, often alone, with some financial and practical support from aid organisations but little emotional sustenance, and with no idea where to go or what to do next.

Some headed for homes that no longer existed, or into hastily erected displaced-persons camps from where they slowly found other places to live. Within months, the first of thousands were making their way across the world to Australia. Despite restrictive government policy — with a quota of just 3,000 survivors allowed to enter in the immediate post-war years, compared to 9,000 in the pre-war period — the nation became second only to Israel as a haven for Holocaust survivors on a per capita basis. From 1946 to 1961, 27,000 Jewish survivors migrated to Australia, more than doubling the size of the country's pre-war community, and irrevocably infusing it with a Central European character. In addition, 170,000 displaced persons who were not Jewish had arrived by 1951.

But distance was no counter to history. So many had been killed, and so many families and cultures decimated, that even moving as far away as Australia could not displace the past. Liberation was loaded, tinged with the guilt of surviving when so many others had not. Lives that had once been an inherent continuum were suddenly split into pre-war and post-war years, and what-had-once-been became a shadow that would accompany survivors for the rest of their lives — even as their outward responses varied.

Some shared their experiences with partners, less often with their children, and frequently found the closest approximation to comfort by swapping memories with other survivors. Some opted to be silent about a recent past that was too traumatic to contemplate, a belief that was strengthened whenever they learned of other survivors being met with disbelief upon sharing their stories with those who had been shielded from Europe's death camps.

Instead, they concentrated on constructing their post-war lives, often marrying quickly to erase loneliness, learning English and working, creating new families. The past continually hovered, but beyond a smattering of memoirs published soon after the war, mostly in Yiddish, a long silence descended. Few wanted to look back on their recent gruesome histories. And even if they did, who else was interested?

It was not until 1961, when Nazi Adolf Eichmann, who had masterminded the mass deportations, was tried in Israel and hanged, that the curtain of silence started to open. Eichmann's Jerusalem trial attracted international attention and belatedly stirred a wider public interest in the Holocaust.

Events that had been too traumatic to discuss privately started to be portrayed on television and increasingly at cinemas. Associations of survivors, and of their descendants, were formed. With the establishment of historical Holocaust centres in Melbourne and Sydney, survivors began volunteering to retell their stories to outsiders.

By the 1990s, many had realised the need to preserve their histories for posterity, even if they sometimes appeared bitterly uncomfortable as they did so. Around 2,500 Australians recorded video testimonies with the University of Southern California's Shoah Foundation, an international program founded in 1994 by moviemaker Steven Spielberg following his encounters with multiple survivors while filming *Schindler's List*. Others recounted their experiences to Holocaust centres in Melbourne and Sydney.

While some resumed silence thereafter, others were inspired to keep talking, sometimes to their wider families but also to students and educators and myriad visitors to Jewish museums, where they found late-life acclaim as volunteer guides willing to discuss the terrifying pasts they had kept hidden for so long.

Speaking publicly became a delayed catharsis for some, just as others shunned the belated attention. As the twenty-first century dawned, the one thing that united the oldest of them was their longevity. They had survived longer than anyone might have imagined. But how had they lived?

'I was educated at Auschwitz. I was three times next to the chimney.' These are the first words uttered for this book, declared spontaneously by a nursing-home resident just before the start of the first of many conversations in multiple cities.

The elderly man who proffers these observations is not preparing for an interview. He is sitting alone, along the route to someone else's room. But time cannot contain an ever-present past from a stranger walking his way. 'Have you ever seen a number,' he asks next, and without waiting for an answer rolls up one of his shirt sleeves to reveal the crudely tattooed digits that have marked him, throughout his unexpectedly long life, as one of Hitler's intended victims.

More than seventy years have lapsed since his arrival at the concentration camp Auschwitz, where his identity was replaced with this very number, and here he is, a long lifetime later, well dressed, well fed, and on the other side of the world with a past he has never managed to elude.

Time has skewed his long years as a survivor, as it has for so many others, making some events seem like yesterday even as the once recognisable faces of long-departed parents and siblings fade.

For many survivors, time has been a slow crawling curse, even as it has assumed a more recent element of urgency. 'Don't wait too long,' the intended interviewee jokes days later, the first of many survivors to utter the same warning, as hours of conversation end with a promise to check back on his chapter as soon as it is written.

Time was always going to stalk this book, given the advanced age of all its subjects, but it would become even more pertinent within months when a call about interviewing one possible survivor leads to an alternative recommendation.

Rezi Ritterman gave her testimony to the Shoah Foundation in the mid-1990s, a two-and-a-half-hour-long description spanning her birth in Vienna, her privileged childhood in Kraków, and the terror of her early adult years when her parents were interred in Poland and then Russia. She spoke of a pogrom where every tenth person was sent to a concentration camp, and how she had survived because she was ninth in line; of having had her head shaved and her arm tattooed in Auschwitz before being marched towards a fire, and ordered in another direction at the last minute; of being forcibly sent on a death march through Germany in the freezing start of 1945, as the Allies approached and Nazi guards ensured their captives, who were being evacuated from multiple camps, kept moving away from the front or else were shot immediately.

She talked about her ongoing regret at having been denied an education; about the enormous family she had lost to the war; of how she had spoken so little of her Holocaust experiences that she had cancelled the appointment to record her testimony three times before she finally sat down before this camera, in her comfortable Melbourne lounge room, to talk about a past she could not even surgically dislodge.

There was a bitterness as she recounted her story in 1996, exhibiting almost physical discomfort as she did so. But now, twenty years later, she wishes to elaborate. She is on holidays when contacted a day later, and in a busy shopping mall where it is too noisy for introductions over a mobile phone. Could we talk when she returns in a few weeks?

Time intervenes as other interviews are completed, and after she has been back for some days a date is arranged to speak at first by phone and then to organise an interview in person.

But she does not answer at the appointed time. On her phone is a message from her son: she is no longer at home and can be reached at an alternative number. In her early nineties, she has been diagnosed with cancer.

She is, however, still very keen to speak, says her stepdaughter soon after, even though the diagnosis is so new. 'Just wait a little longer,' she adds. 'Please don't forget her.' And time intervenes again, and, not three weeks later, Rezi Ritterman dies, taking the burden of her lifelong memories with her. 'It is really sad that she missed the opportunity to tell you her story,' her stepdaughter emails later. 'I think she was very ready.'

Survivors are a fading group. There are perhaps a few hundred thousand still alive around the world, and many of them were children when the war ended. Fewer than 7,000 remain in Australia.

The people interviewed in this book are part of an increasingly rare demographic: survivors of Nazism who have adult memories of the Holocaust. Born in 1926 or earlier, they were at least eighteen when the war ended. Percentage-wise, the war consumed a small fraction of their lives. But its legacy endures in their memories, their outlooks, and increasingly in their dreams.

They are the last living voices of a generation that was not meant to be, men and women now in their tenth and eleventh decades who have defied not just the law of a nation that sought to annihilate them, but the law of nature that not so long ago would have dictated a much shorter lifespan.

Having outlived in many cases almost all their contemporaries, their unexpected longevity has culminated in a quandary where the desire to record their histories has become for many just as intense as the desire to forget it.

They are the last survivors.

Annetta Able and Stephanie Heller

BORN: Annetta Heller and Štěpánka Heller
4 February 1924
Subotica, Yugoslavia

In their long and largely intertwined lives, Annetta Able and her twin, Stephanie Heller, have shared many achievements. They survived the Holocaust when their family did not. They endured most of those harrowing years together. And they withstood the macabre experiments of the Auschwitz physician Dr Josef Mengele.

But it was only at 92, when they had reached an age that was once seemingly unattainable, that they learned of their inclusion in the Guinness World Records. While they had been diligently creating the second part of their lives in a quiet corner of Melbourne, the elders of a post-war family spanning four generations, to their great surprise they had been recognised as the world's oldest co-twins to have survived Mengele's misdeeds.

Every life story is unique, but what makes the account of these sisters so unusual is their mutual experiences. Their survival is essentially one story, not two. At a time when being a Jew in Europe meant losing control over almost everything, they managed to endure World War II mostly together. And, apart from the ten minutes that separated them at birth, and the eight years in which they lived in different countries in the post-war years, that has been the pattern for close to a century.

Happenstance has been a recurring theme of their shared lives. Although their family was Czech, they were born in Yugoslavia, where their mother was visiting relatives when she went into labour early.

The twins grew up in Prague, with their younger sister, Alžběta, their mother, Terezie, and their stepfather, whose surname Heilbrunn they adopted when they were six, in a household that paid only moderate attention to religion. Their mother used the Ten Commandments as a code for daily living. She also ensured that they observed some of the main Jewish festivals.

But despite their keenly Czech identities, the war had an immediate impact. As Jews, they were quickly banned from many public places. Midway through their education, they were no longer allowed to attend school and began living and working at an orphanage, their own childhoods having been abruptly ended.

In 1941, as many families were separated on the basis of suitability to work for Germany, their mother, stepfather, and sister were deported to the Łódź ghetto in Poland. They never saw them again. Alone at seventeen, the twins remained in the orphanage as the tumult of their early adulthood accelerated.

The following year, Stephanie married an engineering student, Egon Kunewalder, in a nondescript ceremony where even photographs were banned. A month later, Annetta was sent to the ghetto in nearby Terezín, which Germany had renamed Theresienstadt, and worked as a nursing aide. Stephanie and her husband joined her there six months later.

Within another year all three had been transported to Nazi Germany's largest concentration camp, Birkenau

(Auschwitz II). Stephanie's husband later died there. The sisters, meanwhile, were taken to the camp physician Mengele, who was conducting barbarous experiments on twins, dwarfs, and Romani.

At twenty, their existence became a macabre mix of work and tests. At times, they were loading naked corpses onto trucks, a gruesome job for which there was never a change of clothes let alone a piece of soap to cleanse themselves. At other times, they were being tested by Mengele's aides, and undergoing countless X-rays, injections, measurements, and gynaecological procedures, until it was clear that they were identical. Then they were transfused with the blood of Polish male twins they had never met.

The procedure was frightening in itself, but, when the blood types proved to be incompatible, the sisters became gravely ill. While they recovered, they never learned the fate of the brothers. Through a friend who had spoken to a German doctor prisoner working with Mengele, they later learned that they were to have been forced to have sex with the male twins. Mengele's plan, which was stymied by the advance of Allied troops, was to see if identical twins could produce identical twins. All four parents and their babies would have been killed by the time the test was completed.

Instead, the sisters were sent on a death march in the bitter opening to 1945, and then to two more camps, before they emerged from an unguarded barracks in March 1945. Sensing that the Germans had gone, they grabbed some bread and blankets, and walked out to freedom.

Their joy at liberation, however, was soon dulled by the realisation that their family had been killed. They found their way back to Prague and studied nursing, and again their lives morphed rapidly. In 1948, Annetta married Jirka Able, a former Auschwitz inmate whom she re-met, post-war, at a dance. In 1949, Stephanie moved to Israel, followed later by her sister and brother-in-law. After a brief second marriage, in 1954, Stephanie married a cousin, Robert Heller, regaining her original family name in the process, and she moved to his home in Kenya until the independence war disrupted their plans to remain in Africa. By 1963, both sisters and their families were living in Melbourne.

Since then, neither has moved more than a few blocks from the antipodean pocket that has become their world. Both widowed, they still live only streets away from one another in an established neighbourhood of spacious homes and well-tended gardens.

They speak every day, often taking over one another's sentences and laughing more often than you might expect. The most common phrase in their lively, lifelong banter is invariably directed to the other: 'Let me speak.'

Annetta

We are very stubborn, both of us. We continually quarrel, but we couldn't be without each other. That's why I am in Australia; of course I wanted to be with her.

When we left the last concentration camp, we had hope that life would be normal again and we would see the family, so we felt like happy people. The guards were not there, so we walked out. At moments like that, it's instinct. We were young. You don't like to think when you have a broken leg that you can't walk. You think, now I can walk, I will run.

We came home with nothing. We had lost most things when we went to Terezín. When we got to Auschwitz, we had lost even more. And when we came out of Auschwitz, we had nothing. Then when we came home, we found our friend; our mother had put in a suitcase some pictures from our past life, the good times, and left them with her. That was the biggest gift we could get. Diamonds you can buy, but not those photographs.

After the war, no one wanted to listen to what had happened, because they wouldn't believe us. And we didn't want to tell them. There was no help, no counselling. It was only Štěpa and I alive. All the family was gone. Very often, we would see a girl in the street and wonder if she was our sister, for years and years.

We didn't talk much about what happened. And we wanted

to start a new life. I feel that I missed a lot, my childhood was stolen, I missed education. So we tried to absorb everything that was missing. We wanted to get somewhere and to be something.

We didn't know how to accept everything about the normal way of life. It was a nice surprise always when I had toilet paper, and I could think about my day and not be burdened with what bad things would happen. Somehow, I was like a bird running out of its cage.

Because we saw so much suffering and we couldn't help our mother, we wanted to help other people. I worked as a nurse until I came here. If I hadn't gone to a concentration camp, maybe I could have had a career. I don't know. If you go from cold to warm, you don't think about how cold you were. You are happy you are warm.

I couldn't be a nurse here because I didn't know English, so I was working as a cleaning lady. I liked it, actually. I was working for a sister-in-law of the prime minister Robert Menzies. She was so nice when the Czechoslovakian uprising was on, putting on Smetana records for me. She was always saying, 'I admire you because you know other languages.'

After the war, everyone looked for someone to make a new life. I wanted to get married and have a family. I had met my husband in a concentration camp; he was carrying dead bodies. I was lucky because we had a common language; he was Czech and I was Czech. We could talk about everything. And we had so many friends who went through the same.

He was very good looking and he was nice. We had a good life, but he was seventeen years older and he had lived a life already, and I was like a little colt kicking and I wanted to change him and I couldn't.

If I would have him today, I would appreciate him better and I would treat him better. I would give my last piece of bread to my husband, but I wasn't telling him each day 'I love you' like people do now, or kissing all the time — maybe because of the circumstances we were brought up in.

He was always third. My sister came first, and then my children, and he was the third. He knew it. We would sometimes quarrel about Štěpa. I did put her first — because she was my blood. I loved him my way, but always Stephanie came first.

The happiest time in my life was when our son was born in 1948. It was a new life after so much loss. And the same when the others were born. I would do everything for them, tried to give them everything possible: fresh air and good food. It was my world being a mother. I was so happy. I would jump in the sea for them.

Many people can't understand, after the problems we went through, how we could start a new life and have joy. I missed so much, so I wanted to fill it in. It wasn't always easy, but I was happy. I accepted life as it came and I tried not to be burdened with all the memories.

Stephanie started speaking to students about the war. She is maybe stronger in that way, and she knows English fluently. Sometimes, she wanted me to come and talk to groups with her, but I didn't feel that I could give them more than they already knew. And I was a little bit more emotional. Even now when I listen to my recorded testimony, which I made years ago, I cry.

I had nightmares at the start, of course. I suffered from migraines until menopause. I had a lot of tummy pain. They said it was psychological. It wasn't. If they don't know what to say, they say it's psychological.

The Holocaust is still deep in one corner of the brain, but you avoid it. You go around it. You don't have to go in. You have to harden yourself not to get the pain or bad feelings because only that way can you get through life. If you put your mind to it, it's easy.

I cry mostly when I think about my mother. Not because of me. I am so sorry that my mother couldn't achieve anything. She was the main support in my life. I remember everything she was saying: 'Think of those people who are worse off,' things like that. That was a big help in my life.

She was very strong, very intelligent, very gentle, amazing, a very special person and ahead of her time. She loved us. She gave life to us. She had to be the strong one in the family. I regret that I couldn't help my mother when she needed it. And I couldn't enjoy her life and she couldn't enjoy everything that I have now. That's my big regret.

Our mother always told us to look at the bright side. And I do. My grandson had an accident yesterday. It could be worse. You appreciate what you have. That's actually the point of my life, why I try to keep my family together. Until recently, I was having them for Friday dinner every week. Štěpa and I didn't have family. But they have family, and I want them to keep together.

I have three children, eight grandchildren, three great-grandchildren and one on the way. I am afraid only when someone in my family is sick; I am afraid of losing someone. But otherwise I am not afraid of the world.

It's a different time today. If you pity yourself and think how much was lost, it doesn't help anyone. I don't want my children to pity me, and they know it. You should be big enough to forgive. If you don't forgive, you punish yourself, too. If you leave it behind, you can start from new.

I am lucky. I achieved a lot. If you take it the right way, it's possible to have a good life. If my mother saw me now, she would be very happy. She would be saying, 'Annetta, you managed well.'

Stephanie

In Kenya, I knew nobody who would have been in a concentration camp. I didn't want to talk about it, because I couldn't explain it to them properly. And I didn't think it was correct for me to talk. If they didn't know anything about it, I wouldn't start to tell them. Sometimes, I would have liked to tell them: 'You make so much fuss about this broken plate and we didn't even have a spoon.' But I kept myself back. I didn't want my husband to feel sorry for me. I told him most things, but I noticed that he started to be so sorry for me, and actually didn't like to hear it.

I didn't forget about it, but I somehow put the past behind me. I was clinging to the normal way of life. When I thought of the past, it was always about my mother and my sister.

There was a great bond between our mother and us. She was the most important person in our lives. She was showing us her love by telling us what we should do to have a better way of life. I think she might have had an idea when we said goodbye in Prague that we were seeing each other for the last time, because she didn't talk much. She just kissed us. 'Look after each other,' she said, and that was it.

When my mother-in-law was sick in Mombasa, the family chose me, because I was a nurse, to fly there and be with her. That was awful; after she died, some ladies made me join them to wash her body and dress her in the orthodox way. And I was thinking, it might have been my mother. That was dreadful. At the funeral, I cried; I couldn't stop, because I thought of my mother. I was lucky that I was able to cry, it occurred to me. And then I cried more. It was the first time I was really able to.

I felt very guilty that we survived and Maminka, our mother, and our little sister didn't. I used to have nightmares, very vivid. I was frightened something would happen to the children. I used to cry in my dreams occasionally, but, it was so bad, I forgot it when I woke up.

I was always worried about my children. When they were born, I was very protective and very strict with hygiene, because I had seen so much death that I was worried if I wasn't careful they might get sick, too.

In Kenya, I didn't let anyone do anything for them. I wouldn't let them take them out of the cot. I let them wash nappies and hang them up, but later I ironed them to get rid of viruses. I was always worrying. I didn't want them to touch things. And later, I didn't let them run around barefoot. I was always after them. I was always cleaning their hands, everything possible so that they wouldn't get some sickness. I was probably more frightened for my children than other mothers, more fussy.

I didn't worry before I was a mother, because I had no one to worry about. I had a sister, she was with me, and I never worried about her, because I knew she was strong.

I had nightmares about Mengele only later. He was the most important to us in the camp, because if you think about it he saved our lives — for his purpose. He didn't save us for us. We were his guinea pigs. You don't kill your guinea pigs if you want to continue your research.

I actually liked him at the beginning. He was not unpleasant. He was not shouting at us. We understood that he wanted to study twins. It made us pleased that we had been chosen for experiments. We didn't know about his plan. We didn't know that everybody was to be killed.

I never thought I wouldn't be with Annetta. I always took it for granted that we wouldn't die. That was just luck. And we were lucky that we weren't experimented on so that it would make trouble for life; a friend of ours was X-rayed and couldn't have children. There were many of them who were crippled.

We have seen good and bad in people. When we came back from the war, we had nowhere to go; we had nothing. There was one suitcase, which our mother had left with a neighbour during the war with photographs and documents. She had kept it under her bed the whole time; could you imagine if she had been caught?

Another neighbour, my mother gave her a new electric iron, and said, 'Can you look after it?' When we returned and wanted to have it, she said Mother gave it to her. She was not pleasant at all. All of a sudden, she was a stranger. If I have something from somebody and that somebody has nothing else, for goodness sake I can be without it.

I am not hard, but I don't show so much emotion. I try to keep it to myself. I learned not to cry at the beginning when I started talking to students. I didn't like to show my weakness. I took it for weakness. And most probably other people thought that I felt sorry for myself.

I saw a girl who was crying at the Jewish museum in Melbourne once. I went to her and I asked her what's the matter. She said, 'I am worried that my grandfather was in Germany during the war.' Was he fighting? She didn't know. But she was ashamed that she was German. And I hugged her and I said she didn't have to worry. I said to her, 'I don't blame you. You are the granddaughter of that man, but you are not responsible for his doing. That's the past. It has nothing to do with you.'

I wanted to make her feel better. And I thought, how could I prove to her really that I have nothing against her? So I took the girl and her teacher and two friends, and I brought them home for dinner. She is the second generation. I wanted to show her I have no hard feelings towards them.

I like to please people and help them because somehow I had the feeling I lost so much education in life, I was never sure if what I was doing was correct. At parties, I couldn't talk about cinema or theatre. I was behind in culture, because we didn't have the chance. I never read Shakespeare in Czechoslovakia. When did we have time? I learned to cook from my mother-in-law.

I was always feeling that I didn't have enough education. After the Holocaust, I tried to get what I didn't have the chance to have. I didn't have sunshine, so I went to where there was sunshine. We didn't know how to dance; I still don't know how to dance. But education was the first thing.

My husband and my children could speak very good English. I wanted to prove to them that I could do what they could do. So I went to school on Saturdays to matriculate. I did prove it to them. And they were quite happy that their mother was not such a dumpling.

Apart from my son and daughter, I have seven grandchildren,

one great-grandchild and soon two. Time goes by and you have a different way of life and you have other people to love. I realise I didn't love my first husband so much. I was a young girl, and he was my first love. He married me all of a sudden. Maybe he just felt he wanted to have somebody because the future was uncertain. I know he didn't love me enough, because half a year after we were married he was having an affair.

If he would be here now, I wouldn't want him. If we had both survived, we couldn't have lived together. And my second husband, I don't know why I married him. Robby, my third husband, was my only love.

We had a plan for euthanasia, but I don't think I could have gone through with it, because I'm clumsy and I don't understand much. He fell down on the street and dropped dead. It was a merciful death. He died the way he and I wanted to, without too much fuss. I cried afterwards, but I was relieved for him.

Annetta says sometimes, and I think she might be right, that she was the romantic girl, and I was the factual one. I am matter of fact. I am very upset if something happens and I wish it hadn't happened. But I can't do much about it.

Before she was married, she was under my wing. I wanted to protect her from anything bad. Now she's in charge. Now she is the stronger one because I had four operations with my back and some falls, and she tells me always what to do and what not to do, and that irritates me. Several times lately, I told her, 'I am just as old as you, I can do what I want.'

Annetta had her number removed from her arm a long time ago. I still have my number. When people asked me, I said it was my boyfriend's telephone number. It's part of me now. It belongs to my past.

I didn't want to show people at the beginning. I felt a little bit embarrassed. I was wearing long sleeves. Now I am not embarrassed. I am not squeamish about what was.

I know that I was there. I don't think about it every day. Sometimes, it might be even a week that I don't think about it. And sometimes, it hits me with some small memory: if I see a film and there's a nice child like my sister. When a child cries, and I haven't got anything to give them, that makes me a bit soft, because they don't have what they need.

There are a lot of things in life that I like. I could stand under the shower for twenty minutes. It has to be nice and hot. Fresh bread with butter. If I could have coffee whenever I want, and put as many spoons of sugar, that's wonderful. We had something in the camps in the morning that was just coloured water. They called it coffee. That was not coffee. Now I have coffee.

I get my hair done every week. It's the only thing I do for myself to spend money. I do my nails myself. I don't buy expensive things, because I was always careful that we had enough money as a reserve. But I always like to have extra underwear. When we go on holidays I take more than I need, because I have it, and somehow that's a luxury.

I have been thinking quite often that we were quite lucky when we came to Australia, not just because we had each other. Kenya was good fun. I didn't even think of going to Prague to visit. There was nothing there, only stones. But I only feel at home here. This is the place I have lived most of my life, for more than fifty years.

Life turned out nice. What was bad and sad, we tried to get over and live quite a full and hopeful life. If somebody asks me, 'Are you happy?' Yes, I am.

Zygmunt Swistak

BORN: 5 September 1924
Działdowo, Poland

Zygmunt Swistak lives with his past in a small suburban apartment in Melbourne, a minimally decorated space of eclectic belongings that track his long and varied life. A portrait of an old Polish man hangs in the entrance hall, opposite some of the carefully executed paintings he has produced in his never-ending quest to calm his soul. A framed photo of his grandchild sits on a low bookcase. Outside, in the tiny courtyard, clusters of plants that he has expertly propagated grow in the spring sunshine.

Not all of his history is on display. His war medals, which he proudly dons each Anzac Day as a member of the Polish Resistance during World War II, are wrapped in an old shopping bag, and his Polish army uniform, which he wears on the same march, hangs in his wardrobe.

Mostly, though, his story remains confined to his memory, his haunting tale of survival tinged with a sad sense of solitude. There has rarely been anyone with whom he has sought to share his past, and even fewer who remember it.

History has rendered him a man of minimal emotions. Apart from choral singing, which continues to rouse his spirit, he is mostly sombre, and the only time his mood visibly lifts, through hours of interviews, is when he talks about becoming a father.

His past remains a significant part of his present, trailing his waking hours and increasingly intruding on his sleep. But while the Holocaust is the defining element of his life, it is a term he rarely utters. And when he does, it is almost invariably about someone else's story. Because he is not Jewish, he says he is not entitled to be counted among its survivors. His story, though, is still hellish.

He was born in a Polish town near the German border, the location of his arrival an unintended quirk of geography that would have devastating consequences later.

When he was one, he moved with his parents and his older brother, Tadeusz, to Warsaw, where his father worked as a police officer at the State Mint. He was an adventurous boy, a scout, and he was very inquisitive, often questioning aspects of life that others around him simply accepted, not least the religion that was practised by ninety per cent of his compatriots, including his mother, a devout Catholic.

He was fifteen when German planes flew over Warsaw in 1939, the announcement of war curtailing his childhood almost immediately. When his apartment building was destroyed in an early bombing, he and his family moved to Zielonka, a nearby town where they had spent many holidays. But the familiar air of leisure that he had always associated with the area was quickly replaced with fear and uncertainty, as he was among a group of young students abruptly loaded onto trucks one day, destined for German factories.

He managed to run before his truck started moving, the first of multiple escapes he staged as life grew steadily worse, and, with his mother mostly bedridden with a bad heart, his father was forced to sell the family's belongings for food.

As the war progressed, he was issued with a new identity card. While his parents and brother were listed as Polish, his place of birth had since been annexed and was noted as Germany. What seemed a humorous administrative anomaly became deadly serious in the first year of the war when he was called to a government employment office and told that as a result of his place of birth, he was an ethnic German, and he would need to join the army or work for the war effort outside Poland.

Insisting that he was Polish, he was dragged away by German guards and sent to a temporary jail, and then piled with other prisoners into a goods wagon, before staging another escape as the concentration-camp-bound train rounded a bend and he jumped onto the tracks.

He made his way back to Zielonka, but feared for his safety if he returned home following his escape. Instead, he moved into a small unit at a local pit mine, arranged by members of the local Resistance who asked him, in exchange, to help smuggle two people across the border.

On his return, however, he was caught by German authorities. Over the next few years, he was moved through multiple camps, loading coal one day, digging graves another, and escaping from a work gang to end up in a forest where he met up again with members of the Polish Resistance. He fought in the Warsaw uprising, was caught by German soldiers once more, and was sent by train with his father and brother to the Dachau concentration camp. He was twenty. By then, his mother had died of heart failure.

After several weeks in Dachau, he was moved with others to the Katzbach concentration camp, at the former Adler industrial factory near Frankfurt, where his brother was beaten to death. Soon after, his father was fatally shot.

With his family dead, and his health waning, he was moved to the Vaihingen camp in early 1945, and then, after a death march that many did not survive, he was put on another train. Of the 100-odd people in his wagon, he remembers only two emerging alive on his return to Dachau.

When he was liberated there weeks later by American troops, he had tuberculosis and fluid in his lungs. In the final days of the war, he had been speared in the groin by a guard who had mistaken him for a corpse, and the resulting wound now caused his lower body to swell so badly that his trousers had to be cut off him, and he was unable to stand up.

His first six weeks of freedom were spent in the concentration camp's hospital. The following two years passed in recuperation at a French hospital in Germany, before he moved to a displaced-persons camp.

He was one of 50,000 Polish-born people to arrive in Australia between 1947 and 1954, working initially as a fitter and turner, and later as a toolmaker. In retirement, he has taught plant propagation and chess. Married for many years, he has been separated since he was eighty-six.

Before the war, before this, I was a different character. I was happy-go-lucky, always. I was the life of the party. When there was a dance or something, I made everybody happy, and I was liked.

I was a hyperactive kid and hard to manage, a real troublemaker. I had to do something, and usually by venturing into something not very good: jumping on trams and trains without a ticket, running all over the place. I was streetwise. My brother was the reverse. He was a gentleman right from the start, clean, well dressed, always reading books.

It helped me a lot being an untamed spirit because I knew how to get out of situations and how to avoid things. I started very early having trouble with the Germans. I was arrested a few times, and I was confident always that I would somehow get out. If I was caught, I was already thinking how I could escape. I was so confident that I thought if the Germans shoot, maybe they would kill everybody else, but not me.

Another person came out of the concentration camp. My character after was broken completely, not only from the loss of my father and brother but how they died. I know how they suffered. It is a tremendous weight on my mind even now that I couldn't do anything about it.

When I survived, I was one of the walking skeletons. In

Dachau, they made a lot of pictures of me because I could walk but I couldn't stand up. On my hips, there was bare bone, no skin. I spent two years in hospital — I went through puberty a second time when I was twenty-one — and I wanted to recover as fast as possible. Everybody was lying in bed, but I wouldn't. I was painting. I was making jewellery boxes. I even created a small theatre group.

Sometimes, I read in the paper about Australian soldiers coming back from Vietnam and how they need counselling and all these sorts of things. Whatever they went through, they got through it with a gun in their hands. I was there hopeless, helpless in a concentration camp and I didn't have any support after I came out. Physically they repaired me, but mentally I had to repair myself. I saved my sanity by painting.

And I started to save my brain from the torture of my memories. I created a barrier to not remember the concentration camps. The barrier was so strong that later, when I tried one night to remember what my mother had looked like, I couldn't, and I was really upset.

I was angry and unsocial. My brother and my father suffered and died in that concentration camp. And the anger was that I couldn't do anything about it. I didn't trust anybody. If someone wanted to be friends, I wondered what he wanted. I didn't have friends for a long time. Except for Janus; he was like a brother. We went to primary school together. We were in the Resistance — to defend our freedom and get the Germans out of Poland — but not in the same unit. He ended up in one of the same camps as I was.

We were the only survivors from about fifteen or more friends. He knew what I went through and I knew what he went through. We didn't talk about where we were. Somehow, both of us avoided this. No good reminding each other about what it was. We could almost talk telepathically. This was the only person who could understand me, how I felt. I would say he was the best friend that I had. He is buried in an army cemetery in Warsaw.

There were others I knew from Poland, also from concentration camps. We didn't talk much about it after. We knew from the pain in each other's faces. They have all died now.

I was not violent before the war. Then somebody said something and I didn't like it, so I would punch him. I lost my temper with a Polish man at the DP (displaced-persons) camp in Germany. He swore at me. We were standing on a staircase and I punched him on the nose and he took a step backwards and fell down the stairs. He was knocked about, but he didn't suffer too much. He reported it to the camp police, and they threatened me that I wouldn't go to Australia.

Even here it happened. When we were going to the migration centre at Bonegilla, other people were looking at the burnt grass and dead trees, and some were crying. Where are we going? Into a desert? When I arrived, I took a lot of air into my lungs, looked around — unlimited space, I can go wherever I want — and thought, that's freedom. I felt safe.

The first job they gave me was in the bush, cutting down trees. Two of us were stacking logs. We had been working hard — I was so surprised that I could do it, that I had strength again — and we took a break. All of a sudden, one of the bosses came and opened his mouth at us. He shouted: why were we sitting? And all I could see in him was a German SS man with his attitude and his shouting. So I punched him. I was taken from there and put in a timber mill, miles away, and harder work. But I didn't mind. I was away from him.

Australia gave me a chance for a new life. I didn't aim for too much. I just wanted to have what I was missing. I wanted to belong to a family. So I got married and I had children. That's the only thing I could do.

Once I was married, I started to have motivation. I plunged into work. I wanted to improve and improve and create something for my children. I was full of energy. I was tireless. I was working full-time, coming home, and I was working at home doing everything. I never called anybody to fix anything. I was electrician, plumber, builder, bricklayer, everything, because I wanted to make a future for my family.

The barrier still worked.

In the morning when I was going to work, I was always kissing my wife, but it was more ritual. I became sort of rigid. When I look at some films today, I see modern families that did not go through the tragedy of the last war. I see fathers cuddling their sons or daughters happily, and smiling and laughing. I couldn't do it. And I realise this and I am missing this.

I am unable to show emotion. I feel it, but I can't show it. I can't express myself easily — sadness or happiness. I think it has had a great impact on my family.

One time, when my three daughters were all little, I put one on my knee and pretended I was a horse, and I was singing a song in Polish. My daughters remember this very well, because it didn't happen often. It only happened once that I threw away these chains that were gripping me and I became myself.

That's why my wife left me eventually, because I never completely recovered from the concentration camp. Still it's in me. Anything reminds me. I hear German music: the German waltz played in the Dachau concentration camp every time there was a row of prisoners hung. My mother died on 2 May — that was my name day. And I was arrested on 5 September, on my birthday.

I had so much hate towards the Germans. My father told me once during the war, 'I think you have a chance to survive.' And he asked me to retaliate when I survived, to do something to the Germans. But I couldn't do it. Not on innocent people, I couldn't. I was looking for those that were in the concentration camp. I was going all over Germany after the war looking for the guards. I heard about them here and there, and I couldn't find them anywhere.

I had great hate. I hated all of them. I even hated those that were born just now. That hate was killing me. I realised this later when I went to Germany. Three times I have been there. They wanted me to lecture at university, at technical colleges about what I suffered in the concentration camp in Frankfurt.

I just went there to tell them what happened. And I met so many Germans; it started to change me. After I finished one talk, a university student wrapped herself around me. She had tears in her eyes, and said, 'I am sorry for what our fathers and grandfathers have done to you, your family, and your country.' Then I started to get emails from students saying that my survival was not wasted and that to hear from somebody who was there, as an inmate in their country, was a different story. That's how I got rid of the hate. I didn't expect that.

I have changed a lot. I can't get rid of the hate altogether — I still have this resentment of anything that's German — but it's much less than I had, and it doesn't kill me anymore.

But in one way, things are worse. Loneliness brought back more memories. Because the older I am, I have more time to think, the more that memories come back and interfere with my sleep, more and more now, in details, and so vivid.

One memory comes into my head and it escalates. I try to think about flowers, gardens, something pleasant, but nothing can replace this. I sometimes get up at night because I know it won't stop. It's bothered me for so long, I've sometimes wondered why I have lived that long. I should have caved under all this, but I haven't.

I killed German soldiers during the Warsaw uprising. I thought about one of the men, that he probably didn't want war either, he's probably got children and a wife at home, and I killed him. I was really sorry. It was nagging at me. But it was kill or survive, and if I didn't kill he would kill me. But it's still on my conscience; according to the Catholic religion, you don't kill.

Do I believe in God? I go to church to sing in a choir, but I don't go to pray. Why should I pray to a God that hasn't done very well at all and created that much suffering on this earth? That's really added to my terror. If he is really for the people, why did he create something like that — the murder of masses of people?

Yes, I was in that holocaust. But the Holocaust seems to be entirely and only what happened to Jews. Millions of Poles died also in various concentration camps, but it was all hushed up later by the communists. Russia didn't allow Poland to talk about what the Germans had done, because we had East Germany as neighbours. All the world has heard the Jewish part of what happened but not from Poland. I think the Holocaust was for us as well. It's the only word for it.

The pain of what happened, I will always have it. I can't enjoy in full anything; how can you when something is bothering you and you have constant pain?

On two occasions, I heard on television Jewish people telling about their experiences during the war. One man was saying that people don't like to hear morbid stories now and when they talk about you later on they say, 'He talks about such awful things.' And he said, 'It helps me but people don't like it.' I know how it was. I always felt that if I was talking to someone that wants to hear it, it took some of the pain from me. That's what the man said on the television. I feel the same way.

My life was not like an average person's. Of course, I know that. I am aware that I have gone through hell. But I don't class myself as anything special. Because I know there were others just like me.

Mala Sonnabend

BORN: Malka Izrael

21 March 1918

Ostrołęka, Poland

The past is an eternal shadow that Mala Sonnabend has kept mostly private. The first and only time she spoke publicly about her war losses, she was 96, a diminutive woman with a small voice who stood alone on a stage, a box of tissues by her side, and related to so many strangers how she had come to lose almost everything she had loved.

Two hundred people crowded into a too-small auditorium in inner Sydney to listen on that grey, autumn afternoon in 2014 as she spoke quietly about her personal war toll: the devastation of her Polish home near the German border, her years of internment and deprivation in four concentration camps, how she had survived a death march but lost almost every member of her family, including her husband and their infant daughter. She spoke evenly, mostly dispassionately, and when she had finished she received a standing ovation.

Since then, unlike some of her contemporaries, she has mostly declined requests to retell her story. Memories still sear. But the war years also loiter. And in the small room of the retirement village that is now her home, and where the items she amassed in Australia during the second part of her life have been whittled down to the essentials, the few papers she has from those war times, and the stacks of photo albums bulging with images of her Australian family, are always at hand.

She does not like talking about the past, yet she lapses into it repeatedly, mostly with stories of kindness: the German man who advised her to hide in anticipation of the next round-up of Jews; the jail warden who would roll onions to her and others when they were locked in cells; the Nazi soldier who shot into the air, rather than at her, so that she could escape deportation; the other soldier who was expected to turn her in for attempting to smuggle a curtain out of a ghetto, but who instead handed her a safety pin from his lapel so that she could continue to hide it under her clothes.

Her story is one of resilience and luck. The youngest of four daughters, she was raised in a Polish town of 25,000, where one in every three residents was Jewish. She attended a selective co-educational public high school and hoped to become a pharmacist.

When Germany invaded Poland, most of her family — bar one sister and brother-in-law who were living in Melbourne — moved closer to the Russian border for safety. In March 1940, she married her boyfriend, Gedale Rekant, and moved to Sokoły, where he was the local pharmacist and she worked as his assistant. Their daughter Miriam was born in January 1941.

Life under German occupation became increasingly restrictive, and, in September 1942, word spread of an impending round-up of Jews. A local priest who was a school friend of Gedale's offered refuge to the young family. But Mala worried that a crying baby would endanger the priest, so instead they accepted the offer of assistance from another man, who lived further out of town with his wife and six children.

That evening, the couple and their baby arrived at the

home, carrying and wearing whatever they could. As the night progressed, the man continually asked them to hand over whatever they had brought until they were left with just a set of clothes each.

The next morning, the host declared it was safe for the young family to leave. But as the trio emerged to daylight, German soldiers appeared from behind a nearby cemetery wall and began shooting. Mala was struck in the arm and kept running. Her husband and baby were killed.

Endless doors were closed on her that terrible day as she begged other families to take her in until eventually one did. But the risk of being discovered forced her out after a month, and she fled to the ghetto in Białystok. While working in a felt factory there, she was rounded up by Nazis and taken to jail in Grodno, near the Lithuanian border, then to Łomża, where she was inadvertently labelled a political prisoner and packed onto a train for a frightening trip to the Stutthof concentration camp near Gdańsk, before finally being sent to Birkenau.

She arrived at the death camp in January 1944, and became known by the number tattooed to her arm, 74260. A year later, with Russian forces approaching, she was taken on a death march through snow-covered streets to the Ravensbrück concentration camp in northern Germany and then to nearby Malchow. She was on another death march when she escaped near Hamburg, hiding in a barn with two other girls for three days until she heard people shouting, *'die Russen sind da'* ('the Russians are here'), and then she was free.

She fell to her knees when she met her liberator, a Russian soldier on horseback who took her into the farmhouse so she could wash and eat, and who signed an old Christmas card that she had found in the house: 'To the girl from Poland, Mala Rekant, from your liberator.' It was all she had from Germany.

She returned to Poland shortly after, but when she reached Łódź she learned that her family was dead. So she left the country for the last time and turned back to Germany, to a displaced-persons camp, and months later, after hearing of an opening for refugees, she travelled to Sweden. There, in April 1946, she married Isi Sonnabend, a survivor who had been married to her cousin. He, too, had lost a spouse and child to the war.

Seven months after their marriage, they sailed into Melbourne, and were reunited with Mala's sister and her husband – her closest remaining relatives.

When I was liberated, I didn't have anything. Many people who were freed in Germany could go into a house and take anything: cutlery, fur coats. I took a card from the house where I was liberated. This is all. I had no change of clothes, no change of underwear, nothing. I couldn't take anything; I was glad that I was alive, and I didn't bother about material things.

Sweden really helped me learn to become human again. For five years, I'd lived from day to day. I didn't know whether I would get killed in the morning, or lunchtime, or evening. And then we came to Sweden and we saw a table covered with a white tablecloth and plenty of food. I couldn't believe it.

I had to learn to trust people. In Sweden, it was all under snow, and I went to a shop and I saw people had left their parcels outside, and no one took them. You learned how to deal with people. You learned to sit down, to use a knife and fork. You were living for so many years just using your fingers, using a mug for everything. Sweden was the birthplace that showed you a little bit of culture.

And Australia was wonderful. It was very, very difficult at first: I learned to speak English only thanks to the radio and the paper; I slept two hours a night. When everything was done, my husband was studying medicine to requalify in Australia, the dishes were done, I took in some work with Hestia, the bra company, and I was making at home button loops and I was getting peanuts for it, but anyway I was getting something.

For three years, we had nothing. Government benefits did not exist. I used to buy bones from the butcher, put in all the vegetables I could buy for a few pennies that were not fresh anymore, and make some soup for the whole week. How did we survive the three years? I don't know. But we were very happy. We didn't have to put bread under our pillow anymore.

We were some of the first people who came here after the war. I remember when I first started telling my story, my sister didn't believe me. She came to me and very gently said, 'Do you know what, we'll go to a doctor tomorrow. I'll make an appointment and we'll try to help you.'

She thought I was crazy. And she wasn't the only one. Everybody that I talked to was looking at me and thinking that I was just telling stories. So I stopped talking.

I lost a whole family through the war. I didn't want to be reminded of what happened and what I lost. Even now I don't like to talk about it. I spoke only once publicly. I was getting old and I thought there are some things people should know.

I still have nightmares. That's why I don't want to talk, because I just can't. What I'm telling you, what I tell people, is not the same as living through it. I saw terrible things. Of course, you can't forget it, but you don't want to introduce it into your new life.

I became pregnant on the way to Australia. And I had the baby here. I was happiest when my son was born, and later my daughter. Because I never thought I would have a family again, that I would have children again.

The upbringing of the children was probably the best part of my life. I put all my abilities and all my life into it. When I came here, I wanted to go and study pharmacy, and my husband said, 'Why do you want to do this? You're raising the children.' I had a very good, interesting life, a useful life, in bringing up the children, in helping them in the early years when they needed help, to stand by them, to share their lives with them. The best times of my life were when the children were growing up and I always knew what was going on and somehow there was a very good understanding between us. I loved them; I loved the fact that I had a family again. And now I have two children, six grandchildren, and nine great-grandchildren. And I can't believe it.

The children found out slowly about our past, the stories in connection with the family, when they were taken away, what we were eating in the camps. We did it in steps. It was not something I would like to hide from them.

We tried to normalise our life, not to live all the time in the shadow of the war and the camps. We didn't talk to them in a derogatory way. We talked about the war, but when they didn't want to eat, we didn't say, 'You have to eat because we starved,' things like that which happened a lot. It turned out to be the right way.

I was thinking if we wanted to create a new life, we couldn't create it on hatred. Isi felt the same way; otherwise, we wouldn't be able to do it. There was a good understanding between us. We supported each other. We talked a bit, but we didn't have to talk much. We knew a lot of things that happened to each other. When we were in the ghetto in Białystok, we were put in the same building, and he would come and talk every day about what happened, and this brought us closer. We knew each other's families. There wasn't anything that we had to find out. We knew without talking. I don't think we would have survived afterwards if we didn't understand each other.

I consciously didn't want the children to be brought up with a negative approach to life. We both had more or less the same idea. I didn't want them to think that people lost all their humanity. There were many people thanks to whom many survivors are here. I thought it's important when you bring up children to think of good things, that there are good people in the world, not only bad ones.

I think people are good, definitely, because I experienced it; I experienced the good and I experienced the bad, amongst Polish people and amongst German people.

When we were hiding in the house in Sokoły, they just took everything from us in the night. In the morning, they said we could leave because there were no Germans. And as soon as we walked out, Germans started popping up from behind the wall and started shooting and so we started to run. My husband was carrying the baby. They got killed. And I was running, and when I looked around I saw what was happening.

I must have fallen asleep later because at one stage somebody touched me on the arm and I opened my eyes and I saw a German soldier in front of me. He said, 'Get up, and I will take you to where the other Jews are gathered.' And I started to run then, I said, 'You can shoot me instead.' I was running and I heard a shot — and it didn't hit me. I was still alive. And I saw the German walk away. He was shooting in the air and not shooting me. He walked away. It's incredible. Some Germans really behaved properly. Even in camp, there were people who were nice to you and people who were not.

Kindness is very important, and thinking of others, and being grateful. When I came home from school on a Friday afternoon, my mother always prepared three little baskets of food for three families who didn't have much. And I always remember those people who hid me for a month in Poland. I couldn't even go back to thank them when I was liberated, because they still weren't safe from their own people for saving a Jew. I can't forget these acts of kindness.

Tolerance is a big factor in your life. I talked to one lady the other day and she told me she was in the war, and I said, 'How can you criticise food then?' In the war, we got a slice of bread, sometimes it was mouldy, but you survived, and you were grateful if you got an extra slice of cold sausage.

I am generally a positive person. I don't want to think of bad things. When I judge a person, I won't think that you've got bad shoes, I'll think you've got good hair.

It has been a good life. A lot depends on how you make it, what you expect. Everything was built around my family, and I expected them to be good people. When I look at my children, I see they have grown up beautiful kids. All of the grandchildren are very nice. I would like them to follow in the footsteps of their parents, and they all do — choose the right company; the value of work and not to depend on other peoples' earnings; be honest to each other. I can't complain about my grandchildren or children.

I consider myself lucky, absolutely. Despite everything that happened, the fact is that I could bring up a new family. I sometimes think, why am I the only one left? Every time I get together with my family I look at them and I think, well there must have been a reason I survived. There is a reason: to create a new family, not to let the family die altogether.

When I sit at the table on a Friday night and I see my whole family there — embracing Jewish tradition, and the little great-grandchildren doing gymnastics, and the five-year-old saying *Kiddush* (Friday night prayers) — I think about one thing. How come I am the creator of all those things? Do they realise? Because I can hardly realise myself.

Shmulik Moses

BORN: Ernő Mozes

11 September 1923

Balassagyarmat, Hungary

Shmulik Moses's war was short — so brief, comparatively, that for a long time he felt he had not suffered enough to be considered a survivor. Yet its legacy endures, not in any physical manifestation, but with the lingering sense of displacement that flooded his soul midway through his war and never disappeared.

He was a young printer when the Holocaust arrived belatedly in Hungary. The eldest of three brothers, he had grown up in Balassagyarmat, a northern town with a centuries-old Jewish community. By the mid-1800s, every third local was Jewish — a statistic that would seem even more startling by 1945, when just a handful of those people and their descendants were still alive.

For as long as he could remember, he had lived with anti-Semitism. As a Jew, he could serve in the army but not be an officer, and nor could he work in the public service or as a police officer. Instead, when he finished high school and there was no chance of attending university because of his religion, he began learning his trade.

In 1942, as war became increasingly personal to Jews in other parts of Europe, his printing apprenticeship concluded and he moved for work to Budapest, and then to a small town on the Danube. By then he had become increasingly involved with a Zionist youth group, Bnei Akiva, which advocated for the creation of a Jewish state on socialist and religious terms, and he had started learning Hebrew.

Within two years, Nazism was rapidly permeating Hungarian life, and he faced even greater and more sinister restrictions. He had to wear a Star of David on his clothes. A five p.m. curfew was imposed. Before long, local gendarmes arrived at his workplace and ordered him to return to his hometown immediately.

He arrived in April 1944, and within a week was ordered to move again, this time into the town's ghetto with most of his family. Within a month, Jewish men aged fifteen and over were being summoned to the local synagogue, where an official from a local military unit announced that they were to be deployed as army labour: either for Germany, or, to save their lives, with Hungary.

In May 1944, he was mobilised into a Hungarian army labour unit. Of his immediate family, only his mother now remained in Balassagyarmat. Within a fortnight, he was taken to Poland, where, armed with a pick and shovel, his life was reduced to a harsh regimen of tough physical work, with little to eat and often no shelter. As a forced labourer, he had some food but never a full stomach, he was regularly reliant on the goodness of strangers for sustenance, and he was often left to sleep in paddocks with cows.

Even his identity was unprotected from the degradations that were ravaging Jewish life around him. With a Nazi-supporting government having been installed in Hungary, he was no longer referred to by name but by his unit number, and his company was sent west. Sometimes working, but mostly marching, he was forced to trek endlessly across the width of

Hungary, and on one unforgettable day he was led though his hometown where a once flourishing Jewish population had all but vanished.

After marching for two months, he arrived at the Austrian border at the end of 1944, confined to a brick factory when not ordered to clean frozen snow from roads, and as 1945 began he was transferred to Austrian authorities, where SS officers now guarded this weakened and bedraggled group of Jewish men.

Only when he saw one of those officers shoot an inmate in the head as he was digging an army tank ditch did he accept that his life had lost its value; if he, too, was murdered, no one, he realised, would be held accountable.

The toll of forced labour and minimal food increased, and members of his unit became increasingly sick with typhus, to be taken out to a field and shot. He was one of perhaps twenty men still alive when he, too, became seriously ill. As the able-bodied members of his company were moved on, he was driven away by truck, and he resigned himself to death.

Instead, he was taken with others to another Austrian town and dumped at an empty school with few to no guards present. After three days, a Russian soldier arrived, and he was, figuratively, free.

He spent two weeks walking back to Budapest, was arrested several times en route by Russians who suspected him of being a German spy, and learned that his father and two brothers were still alive. He returned home, and with the rest of his family awaited his mother's arrival.

In the post-war years, he began working with other young Jewish people surreptitiously trying to establish contact between surviving European Jewry and the Jewish Brigade of the British army, which was quietly trying to help survivors illegally make their way to Palestine, then under British control, ahead of the establishment of Israel.

He lived in Italy until 1954 when he emigrated to Australia with his wife, Rachel, and the first of their two children. They later ran a ladieswear shop in Sydney.

When I came back from the war, I never felt that I qualified as a survivor. I remember, years later, telling my story to someone from Poland, and she said to me, 'You were in a scout camp.' When I heard about what had happened in Auschwitz and in all those camps, I thought, well, I am not a first-grade sufferer.

It was a short part of my life, and what I went through was still awful. When I got home to Balassagyarmat, we still believed that Mother was coming back; she was taken to Auschwitz a week after I left. Slowly, girls started to return from the camps, and they told stories of what had happened. I couldn't find anybody who remembered Mother from the train or from her arrival at Auschwitz — up till today. I saw her last time when I was marched out of the ghetto; I looked back and I thought, well, now Mum is alone. She had nobody in town anymore. And I still feel guilty that I left her.

Later, my justification was that if I had stayed, we would have both gone to Auschwitz. It pacifies me that I didn't have that choice. But I still have that guilt occasionally when it comes to *Yizkor* (memorial prayers recited four times a year).

And, of course, it has had a significant impact on the rest of my life. There's a Hebrew term, *shechikah* (erosion); it's like a cake of soap and you rub it here and there and in the end you finish off with barely nothing. What happened then made me what I am today.

Before the war, we were living in a self-imposed ghetto. We didn't want to, but we felt easier that way. You were with people with whom you felt comfortable. If you ask me how many people we knew in Balassagyarmat who were non-Jews, I would count it on my hand.

We had been part of this war all along in a non-acute way. As a Jew, I couldn't study at university. I couldn't be a public servant. We always dreamed that being in Hungary, we might slip through somehow. We watched the map, how the Germans retreated, and we thought we may be safe.

But we only knew so much. I look today at how Adolf Eichmann took 440,000 Hungarian Jews to Auschwitz in mid-1944, a whole year after the Warsaw ghetto uprising, and we still didn't know about it. We didn't know there was a Warsaw ghetto uprising. We didn't know Auschwitz existed. That's why we went like sheep.

I haven't got enough reasons why we didn't try to escape. Our wagons with the military, when they transferred me to Poland, were open. We could have jumped out. But where could we go?

Later, when I was being marched through my hometown, I figured out that to escape wasn't a big deal. You could lie down in the gutter, and the rest of them went, and you stayed. But I couldn't figure out to whom in Balassagyarmat I could go.

It was November, it had started to get cold, and I speculated, okay, I will escape and I could go to my house. But what do I do if the lady now living there says, 'No, I don't want you'? I realised then that I don't belong here. Nobody wants me.

That sense of isolation I felt from the moment I passed through my town encapsulates my whole life story. It gave me the picture that I am a stranger here. I never felt at home again.

I realised that I didn't have more than two people to try to ask for help. I didn't know anybody. Somehow through the process I became more Jewish than before. Before, Jewishness meant that I put on the *tefillin* (phylacteries) and I went to the synagogue. Later, it meant I was a minority that lives in a strange country.

For thousands of years, we didn't realise that we were guests, tolerated guests in these countries. And we kept on climbing slowly up. They looked upon us as though the Jews have got everything, the Jews are the rich ones. They were waiting to get into our flats. Later on, I saw a suit of mine on a local chap. I asked him when he bought it. He said it was from the local flea market in Budapest: my suit, tailored to my measure, that he had already torn. And I turned to my brothers and said: 'What should I do, start an argument when nobody will support me?'

I felt the impotence of being a survivor. They kicked us in the arse and we still came back begging. When I went home after the war, I felt that they were glad to have been rid of us, and they looked askance that we were coming, seeping back. Their attitude was sort of: what are you doing here? We were still powerless after the war. So I became a Zionist.

Many refugees were coming back from Russia, people who had run away from Poland when the war was on and now they returned and they couldn't establish themselves in Poland because there was open anti-Semitism. It was a hopeless situation. So our people convinced them the only solution for them is to go to Palestine.

The British were against it. They didn't want Jews leaving Europe, so it had to be done secretly. I participated in meetings when some of the future leaders of the labour movement in Israel discussed why Jewish survivors should not stay in Europe. And at the meeting one of them said, 'You have to force them. If they don't want to come, force them to come' — in the belief that if immigration had existed during the war, a lot more people would have still been alive.

This stream of people started to develop through Italy, more or less out of control. They were happy to be saved. They were usually youth, picked up as remnants from the camps and promised safety in Palestine. They were transported by the Jewish Brigade from Austria, from Germany to Italy with the hope that a ship would come and take them across the Mediterranean Sea.

Yes, I was a people smuggler in today's terms. I was comfortable doing it. I felt it was worthwhile, yes. Why did I become involved? That was part of my duty towards my people. I survived. I had to do something.

I was an overgrown member of a youth movement, and in youth movements you talk, you dream. Now all of this — establishing a home for the Jewish people — became all of a sudden a reality. I was working with many like-minded survivors; when the first Israeli parliament was set up, a quarter of the members I knew personally.

But Israel was also a country with a lot of difficulties. So we came to Australia. By the time we arrived, I was a father, married, and I had to provide for the family. I liked that Australia was far away. In Italy, I wasn't allowed to work for an Italian, because I was a foreigner, a refugee. When I came to

Australia, I had only one worry: to make a living, to progress. I went to work within a week. You had to get used to the fact that everything was upside down, much more casual.

I didn't feel at home, but I felt tolerated. I said to many Australians, 'You don't have to love me, but you will bloody tolerate me.' That's a feeling I didn't have in Europe. I felt safe here.

I spoke about the war as often as I met with people. When we had these afternoon teas or dinners, it always came down to 'What happened to you in the war?' No matter how you wriggled, by the time the food was over and you had a schmooze, it always came down to that subject.

Today, some survivors are buying up old houses in the centre of Budapest and building hotels there. I think that's wrong. Once they demonstrate that they don't want you, what the hell are you going to push yourself back there for? Our people are still the minority.

Last night, when I wasn't sleeping, I counted 100 people from Balassagyarmat who survived.

Lena Goldstein

BORN: Chaja Midler

31 January 1919

Lublin, Poland

There are no visual clues to the Holocaust's legacy on Lena Goldstein's long life. She bares no outward scars or wounds, and her arms, though spotted with age, are tattoo-free.

She is a lively woman, sharp and witty, a natural conversationalist. But her words, often and invariably, flow back to World War II, whether she is voluntarily addressing a class of children about her survival tale, a decades-long labour for which she has been awarded an Order of Australia Medal, or chatting otherwise inconsequentially over a coffee. She talks for hours, evenly and in detail, and then laments that there is still so much more to be said. Just as calmly, she flicks through a book of graphic photographs of the Warsaw ghetto, her one-time enforced home, without flinching. 'I am just checking that it was like that,' she says as she turns through the same pages of dead body piles and dying children that have lined this tome, unchanged, for decades. 'And it was like that.'

Her burden is invisible and enduring. Six per cent of her life was consumed by war, a proportion that lessens the longer she lives. But her memory of those six years, and their personal toll, has become her life's longest companion, a weighty presence that has outlasted every member of the tiny circle of loved ones who survived when she thought no one else had.

The youngest of four siblings, she was born in Lublin, where her childhood comprised Polish and Jewish friendships and family gatherings with multiple aunts, uncles, cousins, and three of her grandparents.

By her late teens, she was living in Warsaw and studying law, a field that hinted at a just and cerebrally satisfying life. After her first semester, however, Jewish students were suddenly ordered to sit to one side of the law auditorium at Warsaw University. They refused, and many were beaten up. When those same students were then banned from sitting exams, her legal future was over.

Her early adulthood was a mix of missed opportunities and occasional miracles over which she had little to no control. Looking to study wherever she could, in 1939 she was accepted into dentistry at a university in Brussels. But Germany invaded Poland before she could leave to start the academic year, and one more possibility evaporated.

In late 1940, when Jews were forced to move to a newly walled part of Warsaw, she and her parents were already living in the area consigned to become the ghetto. So they stayed where they were, with the dwindling assets they would later swap for food.

For five years, she escaped death although it surrounded her constantly. She hid beneath a pile of clothes when her mother was seized from a ghetto laundry on Jewish New Year in 1942. Eight days later, when she tried to stop her father being forcibly marched away on the Day of Atonement, she was whipped into unconsciousness. Both her parents were killed. Soon her boyfriend would also be dead, and, she would learn later, almost everyone she had ever loved.

Of the 400,000-plus Jews who had been forced into the Warsaw ghetto, by early 1943 she was one of just 35,000 who were still alive. In a life otherwise drained of hope, she had learned that some other Jews were planning an uprising, and, from the laundry where she had taken over the work of her dead parents, she was surreptitiously passing on German army uniforms and collecting light bulbs — to be used for Molotov cocktails — from forcibly vacated Jewish homes.

But even the possibility of an uprising was not enough to quell her loneliness. Her sister and brother-in-law had been deported to Siberia and had not been heard from. Apart from her two brothers, who were living apart in the ghetto, unreachable and also soon to be killed, she was alone. In April 1943, she walked towards a ghetto wall, knowing she would be shot as she approached. It was preferable, she decided, to death in a concentration camp.

Instead, two guards beckoned to her, and for reasons they never stated, gave her a reprieve: be at the main gate in a few days, with your hair bleached, and we will let you leave.

She arrived at the wall later that week posing as a Polish woman heading for work. She wore high heels and a short-sleeved shirt, the finest of the few clothes she still had, and in her handbag she carried two identification documents in German and six family photographs. They remain her most cherished possessions.

The same soldiers were there and silently they let her pass. It was 18 April 1943 when she exited. The following day, the Warsaw ghetto uprising began, an ultimately unsuccessful attempt at freedom that ended, weeks later, with the ghetto destroyed and its few remaining occupants killed.

She spent the rest of the war in darkness and mostly silence, hiding for eighteen months with three strangers in a janitor's bathroom inside an apartment block. And then for six months she existed in an underground hole with eight others, a blackened bunker no more than two square metres, not high enough for standing, with one small candle and a daily ration of boiled grain among the few markers of the slow passage of time.

In January 1945, she emerged to a desolate street in a liberated but empty Warsaw, where no one was waiting for her and with nowhere to go. Only then did she cry.

Months later, working to find displaced people around Europe, she discovered that her sister, Fela, and her brother-in-law were alive in Siberia.

In 1945, she met and married Olek Goldstein, a fellow survivor who had outlasted three concentration camps. They arrived in Sydney in January 1949.

It was very dangerous in Poland for Jews after the war. But where could we go? Wherever we wanted to go, nobody wanted us. Then my sister and I remembered a cousin who had been sent to live in Australia before the war. We wrote to the Jewish Welfare Society in Sydney and very quickly we heard back; they found him in the army in New Guinea, and he was so happy to have any family left. Everyone else had died in Poland. He sent us permits immediately.

I had two German documents and photographs of my family. That's all I had. Olek had nothing because he came from a concentration camp. We had the passports that we came with.

A few days after we arrived, someone we had just met told us, 'You have to go on Sunday to Hyde Park, to the Domain, and then you will see a little bit of Australia.' So we went to the Domain and there were those boxes and somebody standing on the box and speaking. Everybody was speaking against somebody. No one was pro anything. And here we see a policeman is promenading past, and smiling and talking to other people — and no intention to arrest anybody.

At this moment, I fell in love with Australia. Because I went through German, Polish, and Russian so-called democracy where you were afraid to talk in front of your child because they might repeat what you said and you would be sent straightaway either to a concentration camp or to a Gulag.

It's a different way of life here, in a good way. You don't know what it means when you come from a country where you are afraid to say a word even in front of your children. And you come here and you are not afraid to say the worst thing about anybody. You are free to say it. They might not like it, but you are responsible for what you do and what you say. It's very liberating. And people that have lived all their lives in a free country, they can't appreciate it. They think it's natural.

I want you to hear what I thought about freedom while I was in the bunker. This was written just for myself, a kind of a diary: 'We dream of freedom. Freedom. This word has acquired a magical power and now it means much more than it ever did before … For us, freedom is a word which has become alive. It is our goal and our dream. It is the sky above us and the sun and the stars and the ground under our feet and the air for our lungs. It is a full stomach and a fearless look. It is the end of a hunted dog's existence. Everything that we are missing and everything for which we strive, that is freedom. Because to us freedom means life.'

That was written on November 16, 1944. Four years later, I am in the Domain. And nobody tells me 'bloody Jew'. And I said to my husband, 'You see, this is freedom.'

When we came out of the bunker, Warsaw was completely destroyed. Because of all the bombings, there was no glass, but we managed to find an apartment and in one small room we replaced one window. A group of us started living there.

Some of my housemates met Olek and invited him to come and stay with us. This is what he looked like: Instead of socks, he had newspaper on his feet. He had trousers made of brown paper bags. No shirt but a child's jacket, so the sleeves were coming up to here. Instead of shoes, he had been wearing clogs, but he couldn't walk far in them, so then he found a pair of football shoes, and he was wearing those. He had a sore tooth, so one side of his face was swollen, and the other side, because of starvation, was sunken. He looked like a caricature of a person. I couldn't have fallen for him from first sight.

I was lonely. I wanted to have somebody to talk to. Someone else wanted to marry me at the time, so I had to leave where I was living because I didn't want to marry him, and it was uncomfortable; I didn't survive to do something I didn't believe in. Olek tried to help me find somewhere else to live.

I could talk to Olek, but he was very inward, and he kept things to himself. So I was trying to 'seduce' him, and it was very hard. His heart was still elsewhere. He had a wife and her family, but they had been taken away. He told me, 'Until I know what happened to Lily, I am not going to start any other relationship.' He was going to Lublin, looking for his wife. I warned him, 'There's no sense going to Lublin.' Because I knew that no one had survived there.

He never talked about her, but he must have loved his first wife very much when he lost her because that was his first love and they married in a ghetto, young people, and I always suspected when he is closer to me that he has got a bad conscience.

You couldn't live in Poland as Goldstein; it was too dangerous. So he took on the surname of a dead friend, Okon — nobody had any documents anyway — and we were married at the police station in Warsaw in 1945 as Mr and Mrs Okon.

I don't remember the date; it was a few months after we were liberated. Later, when we were in a displaced-persons camp in Germany and it was safe, we took back the name of Goldstein.

Building a life together was working hard, first of all to escape from Poland, and to start a normal life. And then we came here. First, we were working twelve or fourteen hours a day — I was a finisher at a clothing factory in Bondi Junction as soon I got to Australia — to save for key money. For sure it was not easy, but we didn't feel it. We were satisfied that we were free. Every night, we were going to the pictures, with sandwiches Olek would make, for two or three sessions of the same film. It was like going to university because that was our lessons of the English language. That's how we lived.

We had our own factory later. Then Olek bought a shoe shop. I worked as a secretary at my brother-in-law's factory, and then at another factory as a secretary. I don't remember ever regretting that I didn't go ahead with law. I would be happy if I finished any studies.

For eleven years, I didn't want to have children, because I was sure that if I loved my children I would have to lose them — as I lost everybody I ever loved. When I became a mother, I was afraid to show my love to my two children. I was trying to pretend that I didn't love them; I was trying to cheat fate.

I was doing everything that I should; they had music lessons, they did sport. But I didn't show my feelings to them, because I was afraid. I was afraid to kiss them. When the other mothers were kissing their children, we called it 'chuchela muchela', and I was playing the part of a cold mother.

I am not a compliment-maker. I never repeated to my sons if someone said something nice about them. I was afraid to tell them. Inwardly, I was very proud of them because I never heard anyone saying something unpleasant about them. I should be very proud of them. They are nice boys. But I don't tell them.

My grandchildren, I am the same with them. I can't come and hug them and kiss them. I do feel great love and concern for them, but I can't show it; I can't be open about it. What's the result of it? Let's say they come here, a whole group of friends or family, my boys will kiss every woman hello, but they won't kiss me. I know they probably missed out on the hugging and kissing, but I was afraid to do it.

The most important thing in my life is my personal family. I can't see anything that is more important. My father had three brothers and a sister, and each one of them had children. And my mother had two sisters, and they had children. Only my sister and I survived, and my father's brother's son who was already here.

It's a different world, and you get used to it, and it's no use sitting and saying, 'Look, I could have had here twenty-five people and only have five people.' Some people don't stop talking about the family they lost. Nobody is interested in my little brother or big brother. They are interested in today.

Maybe when I was younger, I believed in God, because my parents were traditional Jews. I am Jewish. It doesn't mean that I am happy being Jewish, because it didn't bring me happiness. But I am proud of being Jewish.

I was already agnostic before the war started. But then I think of my father standing there naked at Treblinka, leading old men saying *Kaddish* (the Jewish memorial prayer) for the women and children that went to the gas chambers just before him. A man who escaped from Treblinka told me that the last thoughts of my father were about me.

And the men standing there were crying *'Shema Yisrael'* (praying 'Hear O Israel') — as their wives and children were being led to the gas chambers — and they were asking God to help them. And there was no answer. And then I read a *Haggadah* (Jewish text at Passover) when they say, every other sentence, *'dayenu'*; 'if we would have done just that and that, that would be enough'. What was enough? That my two-day-old niece had seen so much that she deserved to be killed in a forest? And that's God?

Humiliation, it's worse than physical pain. For the rest of my life, I've felt the anger. In the ghetto, the Germans would catch a young girl, take off her pants, and make her wash the pavement with her panties. It was such a funny spectacle for everyone around, all of our good neighbours. It wasn't funny for us.

When I was hiding in the bunker, I was thinking if I would ever come out, the first German I see on the street, whatever he does, I am going to kill him. But so far, I haven't killed anybody. You are angry. But you can't kill them all. When it comes to it, nobody is able to do it.

You can't put people into one box. Can you say Poles are like that and Jews are like that? There were Jews that were working with the Germans and there were Poles that risked their lives to save people that they didn't even know.

We hoped after the war that people would have learned their lesson and that the world would become a better place. And instead in so many cases it's even worse. People are afraid to go here or there. There were never so many cases of murders. Especially in America, people are going around with guns and shooting innocent people. It was never like that before the war.

People ask me, 'Did you go back?' I don't even know where my whole family was killed. I didn't even have ashes to go to.

I was twenty years old when the war broke out. I had a lot of friends. In all that time, I only once went to a funeral. Everybody was alive. Death was not as constant as it is now. In the last ten days, I went to two funerals and nearly to another one. So many people are dying young.

I don't know whether it's been a good life, but I think in a way I was lucky because I had a good husband and I have got two nice boys, and I have got six nice grandsons, and I have got a nice family. I don't have to live in a chateau. This house is good enough for me.

I live every day as it comes. When I ring my friends up, I am afraid to say, 'How are you?' because they might tell me how they are and that's not what I want to hear. 'I wish I didn't wake up,' that's their usual answer. I don't even think about death.

In the ghetto, we were so used to death that we were passing by dead bodies on the street, it didn't make you stop. This was our life then, people starving to death. I never saw anybody dying; they were taken away from me and then I never saw them again.

When my sister died of breast cancer, I saw her suffering. Then her husband followed her, and then Olek died. Now there is no one in the whole world that I can ask, 'Do you remember?'

Josef Hellen

BORN: 8 February 1926
Hodonín, Czechoslovakia

In a long life marked by extremes, Josef Hellen has been a member of a large Czech family and one of its few post-war survivors. As a young inmate of Birkenau, he was surrounded by death, his own always an imminent possibility, and he became intimately acquainted with poverty. As a resident of Melbourne, he has reached his tenth decade with a private fortune so vast he is one of the most significant Australian property investors in the US.

Working in one continent and living in another, with a love of fast cars and good whisky, his life, in a material sense, is infinitely larger than most. And yet, all this time after World War II, he seems to have never stopped surviving.

He is, by his own assessment, a natural fighter, although there were few obvious signs of that as he grew up in an industrial Czech town, the second-eldest of four children. With a passion for knife throwing, a hobby that he practised endlessly against the door of his family's outside toilet, he was an average student and had little knowledge of the religion into which he had been born. Hodonín, where his father was a butcher, had comparatively few Jews and there was such little emphasis on religion at home that he cannot remember having had a bar mitzvah.

Until he was fifteen, he paid little attention to the encroaching war. Then he was suddenly ordered to wear a Star of David on his clothes, by virtue of the religion that he barely understood. He obeyed the decree mostly, but not on a day in early 1942 when he was one of six boys and a teacher randomly rounded up at school and taken to the local police station, as part of widespread retribution for the assassination of Nazi Reinhard Heydrich, a chief architect of the so-called Final Solution.

He was sent to one prison, then another, and then to the concentration camp Auschwitz, where he was tattooed and his head was shaved, and he was ordered to begin work on the foundations of a camp crematorium.

He worked later in the kitchen at Birkenau, where he was able to supplement his meagre diet, and eventually at the clearing area, known as Canada, where he sorted through other inmates' seized property.

Named in honour of the land of plenty, Canada was a vast storage warehouse, and working there afforded him considerable privilege compared to other inmates. Through the enormous stores of seized goods, he had access to food and clothes, jewellery, and cutlery.

His time in Birkenau was as improbable as his survival. Where others were starving, his access to food meant he was not. From seized cutlery, he was able to alter a set of knives so that he could teach a guard, who had shown an interest in his hobby, to throw them. Several times, he was even rounded up to play soccer beside the crematorium in a team of inmates versus guards, a life-beside-death scenario so absurd he was reluctant to discuss it for a long time.

After working in Canada for almost two years, his life's trajectory changed again in January 1945 when Russian troops were approaching the camp and he and other inmates were forced on a death march. On the first night of the brutal trek, he escaped.

Needing a place to hide, he randomly knocked on the door of a house belonging to an old Polish couple. They allowed him to stay in their hayloft until Russians troops arrived, liberating him and sparing the pair who had harboured him.

The life and death extremes that had marked his survival of World War II continued as he was released back into the free world, a young man who no longer had a family. He took a bicycle and rode back briefly to Birkenau, and with the help of a Russian Jewish captain travelled by truck to Slovakia. From utter poverty at liberation, he was soon working the black market in Eastern Europe, based in Hungary, where he had gone to find a girlfriend from Birkenau. When his lack of Judaic knowledge failed to impress her orthodox family, however, he turned his attentions to a neighbour, and they were soon engaged.

His wife, Judith, was also a survivor. In 1950, they left for Australia – because it was far from Europe, and because it had fewer Jews than the US, and the comparative lack of competition, he figured, was bound to boost his business prospects.

He started working almost immediately for General Motors, bought a milk bar later in a working-class part of Melbourne, and began to amass a sizeable real-estate portfolio, which eventually extended to the US.

In the mid-1960s, his daughter Evelyn, who had been born

at sea two days before his ship docked in Melbourne, became ill with leukaemia. She died in 1968, aged seventeen. He and his wife later had two other children. Now a grandfather, he works six days a week, and, apart from regular tennis games, business consumes much of his life.

I never thought I was a Jew to start with. I didn't know anything about being Jewish, nothing, till Hitler came along and said, 'You're Jewish.'

Did I resent that? When you lose your parents and your brother and sisters and your relations, everybody, what do you think? I would do anything not to lose them.

The war completely changed me from a boy who didn't know anything about the world. The longest I had been was ten kilometres from Hodonín. I didn't have a clue about business, big business, small business.

I didn't have a young life. I never got to be a young boy, because I went to a concentration camp. It was more than a university. It was life education. Everything I learned the hard way, meaning in Auschwitz. It was a very tough school.

I learned to be cunning, to trust nobody — I didn't trust my finger; everything had to be checked and double-checked — and to take calculated risks. I didn't care about anything or anyone. It was me, me, me, me. I wanted to survive.

In Birkenau, I was lucky to get into a commando called Canada. I had a top position, cleaning boots. Everything came to Canada: salami, sardines; the Greeks bought figs. I got more food than at home. Half a dozen sardines bought you luck;

I went direct to the Polish inmate who was working in the crematorium. There they got gold, diamonds, you name it, but not food. So it was an easy trade through the wire; no pleasure, just business.

It wasn't stealing. Stealing was when you took bread from someone who was really hungry, skin and bones, and you took their last portion of bread. When you steal from Germans, that's organising. They stole. I organised.

When you organise, you have to be very, very patient and have good nerves. I learned everything in the concentration camp: what a diamond is, what gold is, what twenty dollars is worth, and so on. I wanted to have a diamond because it was easy and small. In the end, I got plenty. How many? I wouldn't have a clue. I had a lot of gold and so on buried in the timber where I slept. When I went back to find it, after liberation, it was all burned; dead bodies were still lying around.

The guards treated me better than others. Possibly my face was pretty good, honest. Who knows? For me, everybody was SS. The nicest they would have been, or if they gave me gold, I still was suspicious. Only one guard, *Blöde* (Stupid) Heine, was after me. He found me when I was organising — I took some food — and he started with a stick to get me, hitting me anywhere he could. He broke my nose, gave me this big scar on my face. He would have killed me. And another guard came past and said, 'Leave him alone.' Then he stopped.

I started looking for *Blöde* Heine thirty years ago when I had money and I was travelling. I was looking for a long time. My God, I wanted to find him. I would have killed him, easy. I offered money, but nobody would give me information. I went in Berlin to Jews everywhere, and I asked where and how could

I get him? 'Do you know his name?' I didn't, not his real name. How could I go to the police when I didn't know his name? He just disappeared.

I made a mistake. I should have known his name and memorised it.

I kept in touch with one of the SS guards, the one who had stopped the beating. He was pretty good; he used to talk to me in Canada about his girlfriend and everything. I was young and he knew if he told me something nobody would know. I was not the man who would share something. I never, ever pointed the finger to anyone. I wouldn't even dream about it. After the war, I met him once or twice. We shook hands. He wanted to meet me, and in my opinion he was entitled to. He saved my life. How can I say no?

He wasn't much older than me, possibly four or five years. I never saw him do anything bad. When he came to Canada, one guard said to me, 'He's different. He's a gentleman.' He was a gentleman in one way. But still he was SS in my way. Even though he saved my life, my family was gone. That's not his fault. But he was SS.

I escaped the first night of the death march. I was walking like everybody else, with lots of clothes on and six knives. I could have taken thousands of pullovers from Canada, thousands of everything. I took what was the best, and warm.

There were trees, and every twenty metres was a guard with dogs and a gun. I calculated I would try and jump between the trees. If they sent the dogs, I had no problem, because I had the knives and I could easily use them.

I took the chance. I ran through the trees. I saw a pile of straw for cows, and I hid myself in there. Then I went through some villages. I was on the edge of one village, and two young Polish men came after me. I threw the knives, took them out and cleaned them, and then went on my way. I didn't ask questions. And if they were alive or not, who cares? After millions of people were killed, two more doesn't make any difference.

After the war, I was a different man. I couldn't go home. Where was my home? I had a girlfriend in Canada, so I went to Hungary to wait on her. She was Jewish, very religious. I knew nothing about being a Jew, and her family said no, no marriage. What did I do? I married a neighbour two doors away.

I didn't talk about the war much with my wife. When she came back home, I had already been working for five months on the black market in Hungary. I went to Romania for matches and salt. I went to the Slovak Republic with a lot of cigarettes. And I was changing roubles to dollars. That was my life.

I didn't see any kindness from anybody, especially when I came here. I asked for a 200-pound loan; they said, 'You have to have five guarantors.' How can I get five guarantors when I didn't know anybody? I didn't get the money. I started with fifty pounds, and then my wife went to work at a chemist shop, and that's where we started.

There were all Australian working class people in Broadmeadows, and I was one of them, working fifteen-hour days. Sometimes, I was so tired I forgot to lock the milk bar. No problem; nobody robbed it. The Australian workingman knows if you are working hard. I belong to Australia now — not at first; after a few years.

I went possibly twenty times back to Hodonín. My house was still there. I felt nothing. I saw — let's call them school friends. Every year, we went to one of their vineyards, and there we talked about the girlfriends we had when we were fifteen or sixteen. They asked me about the war; I didn't tell them too much. They wouldn't believe me anyway. I know only them from before the war, nobody else.

I didn't have friends in the war. I still don't really have very close friends. I have got a few reasonable friends who are business friends in Los Angeles, but really close friends, no. My closest friend was my wife.

It has been already eight years that she has been sick. Sometimes she recognises me, sometimes not. Today, if she wasn't at home with the two nurses twenty-four hours, within a week she would be gone. I promised her father more than sixty years ago that I would look after her and if she wished she could have a kosher house, the children would go to a Jewish school. I promised. I delivered.

Really, for eight years now, I have been on my own. I have my business, sometimes tennis. Sometimes, I go on the treadmill for half an hour.

The happiest time in my life was when I had enjoyment with my daughter Evelyn and she was going to kindergarten. My daughter was *numero uno*. We had a hard time the first two or three years. I was young. We gave the little girl to an Australian family to look after her full-time for a year, because my wife was working and I was working. My wife was not so healthy then, and this was the decision that I had to make. She was well cared for. Then we got her back and we were really very happy.

When my daughter died, I just couldn't take it. I never cried. Everything is inside. If I could get it out, it would be much, much better. Every day, I was in the cemetery. I made a mistake not having half a dozen children. I could afford to. I just was too greedy, with time and to make money.

I think about my parents and my sister and brother in the night; I dream. When I was younger, I didn't. In September, I say a memorial prayer for them in English. I took that date years ago; I wouldn't have a clue when they died.

Survivor's guilt? Are you kidding me? I never knew what is guilt. I just was lucky to survive. I would kill to survive. That's my nature, to fight.

I am happy with what I achieved in one way: business-wise I didn't dream I would achieve one tenth of what I got. Work is very, very important. It's in my blood. I am still young at heart. I enjoy fast cars. I have all the whisky I need. I've got everything except one thing. I have got nobody to take over my business.

I still don't know too much about being Jewish. I was born a Jew, and I stick to it. If I would have been born Christian, I would be Christian, I wouldn't change. The religious Jews who survived and who saw people going to the crematorium, they never came back to be religious again. I didn't know anything about being Jewish — and now I am more Jewish than before.

I saw Jews go to the crematorium, 100,000 of them, and I said to myself, I am here two-and-a-half years, and I survived. My family was completely wiped out because they were born Jewish. What the hell, I am the last Mohican.

I am a Jew.

Marianne Schwarz

BORN: Marie Gross

8 August 1922

Vienna, Austria

In a long and cruel war that removed almost every semblance of normalcy from her once civilised world, Marianne Schwarz only lost hope once. She was in her early twenties and an inmate of Germany's Bergen-Belsen concentration camp, the latest in an endless chain of camps in which she had been imprisoned for her entire adulthood simply because of her religion.

Judaism had played a moderate role in her early years in Vienna, where she attended a local school and had had mostly Jewish friends. Her father had been a banker and had then run a haberdashery shop. Yet the religion into which she was born had become the defining element of her existence as Hitler's power increased.

Her mother had wanted to move to Palestine, but her father, nineteen years older, had worried about surviving in another country, with a different language. So they had remained in Vienna, where she watched tearfully, in March 1939, as her only brother, Heinz, seven years her junior, was put on a train to France — and though the childhood he knew was halted, his life was saved.

Banned from attending school because of her religion, in her late teens she tried to find a job with the local Jewish community's retraining program, and spent a few months attending mothercraft and kindergarten courses. She also worked as a nursing aide in a Viennese Jewish hospital.

Yet any outlet she sought soon had limited options as the restrictions on almost every area of her life tightened. As a Jew, she could not be treated by a non-Jewish dentist. She could not use public transport. She could only live in a defined area.

By September 1942, with Jews being deported almost daily, tension among those remaining in Vienna was acute as they awaited news of the next steps of lives that were no longer under their own control. When she and her parents were finally packed onto a train and sent to the Theresienstadt ghetto near Prague, just a week after her grandparents were deported, the relief she felt at the end of so much uncertainty was short-lived.

Her grandfather died at Theresienstadt, and then her father and her grandmother were gassed at Birkenau, where she, too, was sent in May 1944. There she had a number crudely tattooed on her arm, and with other women she was forced to parade naked in front of the camp's infamous physician Dr Josef Mengele.

Apart from her mother, Grete, who was to be with her throughout the war, from Theresienstadt to Birkenau and on to multiple labour camps in Germany, the constant presences in her life were misery and uncertainty. And yet she remembers this time not just for its tragedy, but also for it humanity: reciting poems with other women; the humour that sustained them; and even the New Year's Eve concert for inmates and guards at a German labour camp in which she participated in the last hours of 1944.

In all that time, her faith in people, and in her own survival, was strong, even as her family was slowly eliminated and she was once beaten so savagely by a guard — for having asked if her mother could remain with her while being transported between camps — that she thought her head would be split open.

It was only in Bergen-Belsen, the last of the many camps in which she was imprisoned, that her optimism failed and she was overcome by apathy. Stricken with lice, exhausted and starving, she developed typhus. Gravely ill and weighing thirty-one kilograms, she lost her will to live.

It was mid-spring of 1945, and in her debilitated state she had little awareness of the arrival of the British troops who liberated the camp on 15 April, shocked to discover that most of its 60,000 survivors were barely alive.

In the days that followed, she remembers being stretchered away, her fever dangerously high, and crying out to her emaciated mother who watched on silently but was not allowed to accompany her to a makeshift hospital.

When she had recovered slightly, but was still weak, she headed back out into the camp, days later, hoping for a reunion that never happened. To her continuing regret, her mother survived the war only to die days after she was free.

With her own health still precarious, she was sent to Sweden, with the help of the Red Cross, and once she had recovered she started working there as a nursing aide. Within six months, she had gained twenty-five kilograms. Within another six months, she was preparing to sail to Melbourne, where an uncle and aunt had taken refuge in 1939.

She arrived in Australia in November 1946 and moved in with the couple, sharing a room with their newborn baby. She spent the next two-and-a-half years working as a nanny before returning to Austria in 1949 to marry Joschy Schwarz, whom she had known in Vienna before the war. They settled permanently in Melbourne in 1952.

Hoping to fall pregnant, she stayed at home for many years and raised her only niece while her husband, sister-in-law, and brother-in-law went to work. She had six miscarriages and gave birth to a son, prematurely, in the late 1960s, but he lived for only five days.

After training as a welfare officer, she worked at the Children's Court in Melbourne, and spent many years caring for her husband before his death in 1995.

Now retired, she plays bridge and table tennis multiple times a week and calls bingo monthly.

When the liberation came, I had typhus. I was so sick, I didn't even know we were free. I came to a few days later in a makeshift hospital, and the girls in the room said, 'Don't open your eyes so much.' I was so skinny, you could see only eyes in my face.

When I was a bit better, I went from barrack to barrack with a blanket around me looking for my mother. Whatever happened to me does not compare to that loss of my mother after liberation. I still feel guilty that I couldn't do anything to save her, that she had to suffer all through the war, and then die.

Many people were very kind. One of the English liberators asked me to come with him to the pictures. Maybe he felt pity for me; the way I looked, he couldn't have seen me as a desirable object. A soldier from Belgium gave me a book, *Steppenwolf* by Hermann Hesse. I still have a copy of it. It was a wonderful thing because I used to love reading as a child. That was the first book after the war that I read.

Though I lost my mother, I felt fantastic. I felt I was given back to life, or that life was being given back to me. When I came to Sweden, they asked me if I would like to work in a sanatorium for tuberculosis. I had a friend who worked there, too, and I remember one day we went through the corridors with a comb and a piece of paper and we made music. I felt like

I was coming back into existence. It was a wonderful feeling. The losses were always with me, but life goes on. And I was young. I wanted to live.

One day, I went swimming in a beautiful lake in Sweden with my friend. She still had her mother then, and after a few strokes she said, 'I can't swim anymore.' She suddenly panicked in the deep water, she was hanging on to me, and she pushed me under. Luckily, in the end, she made a few strokes and we were back on land. And we never talked about that with anybody, because it was such a terrible thing; if she had drowned after the war, how would I have told her mother?

My experience in concentration camps taught me a lot of things: resilience, to take people the way they are; and my attitude to life and death is completely different. I am a fatalist. I hate it when people say to me, 'I didn't deserve that.' Who gets what they deserve? Things happen to people, and it's just your attitude and what you do when you are given misfortune that counts.

Nobody wants to lose their life, unless they are really depressed and down. Our greatest urge is to live. I didn't allow myself to be so down that I didn't want to live anymore.

The people that really dropped their bundle, they went because they gave up. Once you gave up, you were gone. In the labour camps in Germany, we were pushing heavy loads of sand, we shipped bricks, everything. We did really hard work. And while we did, we laughed and we told each other jokes. We wanted to show the Germans that they couldn't humiliate us to such an extent that we would lose our dignity. We wanted to show them that they couldn't squash us.

Humour is very important. It keeps you going. When I had

my number tattooed on my arm, of course it was traumatic. When it was on, I don't know how long after, I remember saying, 'That will go nicely with an evening gown when I come out one day.' Deep down, I felt they were not able to take away my identity. I still was the same person.

I really had close friends during the war. It was very important, to share my feelings. We were on the rollcall in Auschwitz in the morning, four o'clock; I stood with a Czech girl and I recited German poetry to her, and she recited Czech poetry to me. My mother was standing also at rollcall — we were really starving — and exchanging recipes with women of her age.

When I came to Australia, it was not so fantastic at first. In Sweden, they have the most wonderful forests, and when I came here I was missing it terribly. Everything was different. But I wanted to like it, and I made myself like it.

I had an urge to talk straightaway. At first, I could only speak to people who shared the same experiences with me because I thought they understood. I talked a lot, but privately. And I think it has made me a good survivor. Because I shared my experiences with people who went through the same things as I did, it seems that I was not touched so badly psychologically.

I met many who were very badly affected. I had a friend, he wrote a book about his past, and he was obsessed with what happened until he died. He had nightmares. He was one who became very bitter.

I didn't become bitter. I tried never to lose my faith in people. I believe in people — although it's not easy. And you know I still bare no deep resentment against the German people today. I refused to believe that everybody was terrible — and they were not.

In 1949, I went back to Vienna to get married. I had had a boyfriend in Theresienstadt, and while I was in Sweden I found out that he had died in a concentration camp, and I really was grieving. No way was I going back to Vienna. I wanted to start a new life.

Then Joschy started writing to me when he heard that I was alive. Everybody said I was crazy to go to Vienna, and to a man with whom I had never had a real relationship. I was very apprehensive going because of my memories. I lost my parents, and nobody was there anymore. But as you see, I am an optimist. And it worked. We were very happily married for forty-six years. And we had not a bad life there.

Before the war, my mother had left some of my clothes with some people who ran a delicatessen in Vienna. The woman, when I came back for the suitcase, said she didn't have them anymore. And then I saw her daughter wearing something made of the material of one of my dresses; apparently, she made a blouse for her out of it, and I resented that very much.

But thinking back, I don't blame her anymore. They were probably not that fantastically well off, so she made her daughter a blouse out of my clothes. It was years later. She thought I would never come back and I wouldn't need it anymore. I don't know how happy she was to see me. She was embarrassed.

I learned to live with what happened to me. It never left me until today. You know I am still reading books about the Holocaust, maybe even more than before. I wouldn't call it an obsession, because I read other things, too. But I am still trying to understand how people like Germans, with culture and music, were capable of doing such a thing. Do I have an answer? No.

I always thought people were good. But the problem is that the majority of people are bystanders; they are a little bit indifferent. You should see what is right and wrong. But it's not easy to stand up, believe me. If I would have been in that same situation and it would have endangered my life, would I have been able to stand up? I don't know. And that's why I hesitate to blame everybody because I don't know how I would have reacted.

I don't believe in God anymore. How can a God permit things like that, for goodness sake? Nobody can be so bad to deserve it. Religion causes an enormous lot of damage all over the world. It stresses the differences between people and it makes everything a lot worse. Similar things are happening today that happened then. I am shocked still today what people are capable of doing to other people. People don't learn from their mistakes, not really.

I dream occasionally. I have sometimes nightmares that my niece is drowning. But in my nightmares, the people I love survive. Nobody dies in my dreams. I don't let them.

There's one more thing I want to tell you. When I was in the labour camp in Germany, I went to the latrine in the middle of the night. It was the most beautiful starry sky. And it consoled me in a way, that the war was going on and the moon and the stars were still around and during the day the sun was shining. There was madness all around, but I looked up and the sky had not changed. Life goes on.

I am satisfied with what I have achieved. I don't think that under my circumstances I could have done anything different. I am alive. I have to laugh.

Life, I find, is still a wonderful thing.

Michael Matz

BORN: Moishe Matz

12 January 1923

Wilno, Poland (also known as Vilna;

now Vilnius, Lithuania)

Michael Matz obscured his past so well and for so long that for many years it seemed his life had begun in Newcastle, Australia, in 1952. In fact, he had been born thirty years earlier on the other side of the world, to a large Jewish family and an old culture whose legacy would linger through his long life.

But the war so devastated his past that the best way to counter its aftermath, he figured, was with silence. He spent three decades working at BHP's Newcastle steelworks, with few opportunities to converse in his native Yiddish and even fewer to exchange stories with survivors, had he so desired. By the time he retired, he had belatedly anglicised his birth name, Moishe, the distinctly Yiddish name that was one of the last outward pointers to his past, and he was looking forward to an easier future.

Time and age, however, wore down the defences he had spent his post-war life constructing, and history began to escape his self-imposed containment lines, seeping into his dreams and his consciousness.

When he speaks of his former life now, which he does willingly but not happily, it is in a long and continuous flow. His gaze is slightly askew, and his expression is mostly sad as he sits in his favourite chair surrounded by dozens of bits of paper on which he has scrawled in his shaky handwriting as many Yiddish words as he can remember. Then he rises slowly from his favourite chair, rustles through a dresser drawer of CDs, selects one, and the sound of old Yiddish songs fills his small lounge room.

In a language that no one around him can understand, he sings of love that can burn and never end, of a heart that can yearn and cry without tears. He sings loudly and with gusto, oblivious to the volume and the noise that is spilling out onto the inner-city street, and only then, as his eyes well and an enormous smile spreads across his face, does he exhibit joy.

He is a child of Wilno, now Vilnius and the capital of Lithuania, but when he was born there in 1923 it was a Polish city whose tens of thousands of Jewish inhabitants ensured that Yiddish was widely spoken. His father was a printer, his mother fairly observant, and he had two brothers and two sisters.

He began working as an apprentice locksmith at fourteen. He was still in his teens when Germany occupied his town, and he saw the first of many roundups of Jewish families, dragged from their homes and sent to nearby Ponary, where more than 75,000 people would be massacred between 1941 and 1944.

Somehow, his house was missed in that first round-up, but before long he and his family were forced into the city's ghetto, where they moved into his grandmother's empty house; she had already been taken to Ponary and was presumed dead.

His job in the ghetto, offloading 100-kilogram bags of potatoes and flour for the German army, was considered vital, and protected him temporarily from being deported. But as life for Jews steadily worsened, a neighbour arranged for him to travel by truck to another town, Lida; in their last conversation, his mother told him she thought he would be safer there.

A massacre in 1942, however, quickly changed that notion. Of the 7,000 Jews thought to have been in Lida, he was among 1,500 to have survived. Lida's ghetto was liquidated in September 1943. He spent a week traipsing through forests, and arrived back in Wilno to learn that his parents were gone, and much of his family.

He was later rounded up again and sent to Estonia to work in brown-coal mines, and then taken by ship to Germany, arriving in August 1944 at the concentration camp Buchenwald, where he was eventually liberated by US troops.

After the war, he planned to return to Wilno. But when he heard that there were no more Jews there, he headed instead for Łódź, and then a displaced-persons camp near Munich, with plans to move to Israel. Instead, in 1946, he met a local woman. They married in 1951, and arrived in Australia in 1952 with their young daughter.

The only other surviving member of his family, his brother Eliezer, died in Israel in 2015.

I had a hard time after the war, a very hard time, very lonely. I had no family; I feel guilty even now about being the last one alive. I can remember a little bit about what my family looked like; I don't have any photographs. My mother was a thin woman. My father was not fat. The older sister was like a mother. She married a teacher from school. Sometimes, I see people who look like my younger sister.

Afterwards, I didn't think much about the things that happened. I didn't dwell on the past. I wanted to make a new life, to make up for what I had missed when I was young. I had to catch up on girls, on food — in the beginning, we were mad about eating — dancing, having a few drinks.

I moved to Bad Tölz, in Germany, and stayed for five years. A friend of mine, a Holocaust survivor, was doing some business there, and I rented a room; it was more like back-to-normal life than being in the DP camp. We had a little Jewish community there of survivors, a synagogue; I worked in a Jewish socks factory. We had a group, Jewish boys playing up a bit, having a drink and going to the dances. We had everything we wanted.

I never thought about getting married. I just thought about having some company, having some sex. But I couldn't get a Jewish girl. I had had a girlfriend in the camp, and after the war she found me. We spent about a week together, then she went back home and wrote me a letter: she had a bloke, much older, and he had come looking for her. She didn't want me, because the Jewish girls were looking for a rich Jewish man — some were more successful than others on the black market. But I didn't have much luck; I wasn't rich. And the next girl — Otti — didn't worry if I was rich or not.

I had seen her walking on the street. She lived in the same town, and one night we met near my place, it was nearly midnight. Of course, I liked her. I was thinking about going to Israel when she asked me to marry her.

I said, 'I can't marry you. You're German.' Then we both started to cry. She said, 'Why not?' I thought how could I marry a German girl after they'd done all the things to us? But she had nothing to do with it — and I liked her; she was the real thing.

Did her family accept me? Yes and no. Her brother didn't trust me at first. But later, it was okay. Both her parents had died, and her sisters were pretty good. They never mentioned the Holocaust. We didn't want to upset the relationship by talking about it.

It was not an easy time for us after the war, because some people were against our relationship. 'How can you marry a German girl?' They didn't actually say it, but I could see it in their reaction.

When we came to Australia I met a nice Jewish lady. She said, 'You will have difficulties.' We did have difficulties. We had an Australian neighbour who used to call Otti 'the bloody SS wife'. Once we were at a party for a Jewish boy, his mother was there and she asked my wife, 'Where do you come from?' And my wife said, 'I come from Germany,' and the woman's face dropped and that was the end of the conversation.

It was harder for her than me after the war. I was tougher. She wanted to come to the synagogue with me, but she wouldn't go, because people looked down on her. We both had bad things said to us, but we got over it. It was hurting, but later on we said we won't react, we won't lose any sleep over it. As long as we're together, that's the main thing.

We started to build our lives here in Newcastle. We would have had the option to go somewhere else, but we were lost — we couldn't speak the language — so we just stayed.

There was nobody to welcome us; they just put us in a camp in Nelson Bay, gave us a job, and we started from there, everybody for himself. I had to get up at four a.m. to get all the way to work. We didn't have enough money to buy a chocolate at first; we couldn't afford to buy fruit. But I had a job, what a beauty, and wages and money. Then we started to live.

The steel works had about 12,000 people. There was one Jewish steel worker that I knew of — me. All my friends at work were Ukrainian, Polish, Russian. I had no Jewish mates at all.

They all knew I was Jewish. There was a Polish bloke I worked with who said, 'God punished the Jews in the war for their sins.' I got really angry with him. I didn't hit him; you would get the sack for hitting him. I just said to him, 'Don't you talk to me anymore.'

I secretly wondered about some of the people I worked with, what they'd been up to during the war. There was a Russian; we used to knock around together. I said to him one day, 'Another bloke told me you were really a German, and that's why you came to Australia.' 'No,' he said, 'I wasn't working for the Germans. I was only wearing their uniform coat. It was wintertime, cold, and I got a coat from the Germans; it was nice and warm.'

I didn't believe him. If you eat onions, you smell; if you did nothing wrong, why didn't you go back home? But what could I do? We worked together day by day. I couldn't find out the truth.

It would've been nice if there were more people to talk to, more survivors. There's only me left now. Not long after I came here, I was in Hunter Street and I saw a jewellery shop, the name was Solomon, so I went in and the owner was an old man who came from Wilno and he could speak Yiddish. It opened up my life. He could tell me how to get a bus, where to go.

Yiddish is such a sweet language. It melts my heart. There were never many people in Newcastle I could speak to. They could say some words — '*chutzpah*' — but everyone was speaking English. Now there's only two people I can still talk to, both at the synagogue.

I wrote my story in Yiddish a few years ago and then translated it into English. I printed a few copies and gave them to everybody. One lady bought five copies. She paid me for them, but I didn't want the money. Somebody had to put it down in writing, to shut up the deniers.

In the beginning, I didn't talk at all. But later on, it all comes out. Bad things I remember more than good things. I didn't do an interview with Spielberg, because I was very sick; I used to get a lot of chest pains from the smallest thing.

I don't believe in God anymore, not really. After the war, the American army came to Buchenwald, and the army rabbi came and made a prayer service. They gave us each a little book, and I said, 'I will go reluctantly because God didn't help us.' We just prayed. They said, 'We will pray to God because we are still alive,' and I said, 'Yes, but many are not alive.'

Till now, I go to the synagogue every week, not because I'm religious but for company, to meet people, get out of the house, find out the news.

I never regretted coming here. It's the best country ever. The only thing is, I wish I were younger. Now I've got everything I want. Money is no object now. My wife gets a pension from Germany. I get a pension from Poland. I got the first payment last month, after seventy years. I can't enjoy it though; what can I spend it on now? I've got a car. I've got money in the bank. I just fixed my teeth up; I put in a denture for the first time. I just painted the house. I put in a roller door.

My life out of ten? Now you talk like a doctor. I am quite happy. I would give it ten. I enjoy what I do. I enjoy my food. I enjoy my little jobs. I potter around in the garden, water the lawn — that's about all.

I think about the fact that now I can have whatever my heart wants, good things like herrings. But I still can't eat more than my stomach will take. When we go shopping and people buy and buy, I say to my daughter, 'Look at this country; you can get whatever you want.' I had nothing and now I can have anything. I can't get over it.

I've got no hatred of anybody. All the things the bastards did to us, I don't dwell on it, otherwise you would go crazy. But I remember the war every night. The dreams are terrible. I dream I go in the forest and I try to hide under a bush and I can't go there, there's somebody else there. I wake up, walk around, and go back to sleep.

Talking has a reaction on me. Last night, after we spoke, I couldn't fall asleep, I had to take some medicine at ten o'clock. I will think for a little while after I finish this interview, but then I'll try to forget. I will have to forget. You can't think about it all the time. It's no good for you. What can you do? The people are dead. They don't feel anything.

Nobody can understand what I have gone through. Nobody will ever understand. But I try not to think about it. You've got to get on with life. You can't change it. You've lost everybody, and that's it.

Rina Schuldiener

BORN: Rivka Perl

28 April 1922

Sucha, Poland

Rina Schuldiener did not stop mourning. Not when she was shoved away from her Auschwitz-bound parents as they were being expelled from their Polish hometown in July 1942, and her life was spared because of her youth. Not when Russian troops crashed through the double row of barbed wire that encircled the last of three forced-labour and concentration camps into which she had been enslaved, and the freedom she had lost in her teens was returned to her as a young woman. And not even as she became a mother, and added a new generation to a once vast extended clan that had been otherwise extinguished.

She mourned even amid the joy of birth, as those first post-war lives were joined by a second generation and then a third. War had stolen her youth, curtailed her education, and claimed the lives of fourteen members of her immediate family. And even though the Holocaust was over, there was little about her cumulative losses that would be reversed as life continued.

Survival did not bring her happiness. On the contrary, it filled her with a sense of sorrow that has never dissipated, lingering longer than any of those she loved first ever lived.

In her post-war life, she has had many long associations. She was married for fifty-two years. She has been a mother since 1947. Sadness, however, has been her longest companion.

It has accompanied her across continents, to her final home in Australia, through a brief stay in Israel that filled her with a sense of place she has never quite replicated, and all the way back to the Polish town where she had only ever lived until others took control of her destiny.

Sucha was an industrious place with a population of 6,200, almost ten per cent Jewish, an important railway junction near Kraków. She grew up there in an orthodox home, the seventh of eight children. Her father prayed at the synagogue twice daily, and her mother covered her hair with a wig in accordance with Jewish modesty requirements. From the multi-storeyed building in which they lived and worked, her parents ran a building-materials business, which at one stage boasted the town's only telephone.

Anti-Semitism had been a fact of life for a long time as it had been in much of Poland, but, after Germany invaded in September 1939, the impediments facing Jewish families became increasingly sinister. Among a series of measures, businesses were overtaken and Jewish residents were required to report to police daily.

To avoid the crackdown, Rina, her parents, and her four brothers who were still at home grabbed a few belongings and fled to a distant town where one of her married sisters was living. When that part of Poland was also overrun by Germans, they went home within weeks, only to be ambushed on the return trip by German soldiers who threw away the family's few remaining pieces of property and taunted Rina's orthodox, bearded father.

Back in Sucha, the family's home and business had been ransacked, and the contents stolen. They survived that freezing winter on carrots and potatoes stored in their cellar, and remained there, with an ever-increasing number of exiled Jewish families from surrounding areas, until 1942, when they were all evicted.

The family moved next to an isolated shack with a mud floor and slept on straw-filled sacks through endless cold nights until July 1942. Then they were rounded up in a local square with other Jews from the region; Rina's parents were among the older adults, along with children under fourteen, sent to Auschwitz. With other young people from the area, Rina was instead sent to a local brewery, which had been converted into a labour camp inside the Jewish ghetto, and from where she was forced with little food to dig ditches, carry rocks, and clean toilets with her bare hands. Her long slide into humiliation was underway.

It continued as she and a group of seventy young Jewish women were taken by train to a flax factory in Freiberg, Germany, where they were made to lift soaked linen from an acid solution with forks, and later shifted with them to another camp in Egelsdorf, where they lived and worked in a locked factory under constant guard.

As 1945 dawned, they were moved again, this time on a days-long march in harsh weather and with no food, escorted by dogs and armed German guards, to the Kratzau concentration camp in Czechoslovakia. The conditions there were foetid, with open bowls of human excrement lining parts of the camp in the absence of almost any latrines. In three months, not once she was able to wash herself.

By the time Russian troops crashed through the camp's perimeter on 9 May 1945, she was covered in lice, she had been severely beaten by a guard for having worn a skirt under her thin dress for warmth, and she was seriously ill with bronchitis. Years of hunger had also taken a massive toll. With her coat on, she weighed thirty-four kilograms.

When her health improved, she headed home to Sucha with six other local young women, hoping to find a single relative alive there. She did not. Instead, she visited the local photographer's studio and scoured countless old proofs for any images of her family. She located a single frame of her mother, date unknown. It remains among her most precious possessions.

Although the war had ended, there was still no peace to be had for the seven Jewish women from Sucha. Tipped off about an imminent anti-Jewish pogrom, they fled again, this time to Germany, where one of Rina's brothers had survived. She later learned that a second brother was also alive, having spent the war in Russia. In a family that had boasted innumerable aunts, uncles, cousins, and grandparents, only they three were still living.

In the months after liberation, she met Sam Schuldiener, a Polish survivor who had lost his entire family. They married in January 1946. The following year, their twins were born.

The young family remained in Poland for twelve years, unable to leave because of the new rules of communism. In 1957, they emigrated to Sydney to be with one of Rina's brothers. She worked for several years on the assembly line of a cosmetics factory, beside a concert pianist and an architect, and later for a bank.

Her extended family now spans four generations and includes several noted academics.

I used to be a happy girl. But my life finished when the war broke out. I was always miserable after. I never recovered.

I can't laugh. I remember myself laughing before the war as a girl. But then came the Germans, and they put up a billboard: 'Jew, the laughing will vanish for you.' And it did. They succeeded.

Before the war, I didn't have to look after myself, absolutely not. I was the only girl at home and four brothers. Maybe I had too good a life before the war. I was spoiled. All I was doing was reading books. The girls in my family were brought up to make *challah* (plaited bread) and have a husband. I should be more educated. Absolutely, it still bothers me. I missed out.

Everybody always knew we were Jewish, not Polish. I couldn't forget that, because I was called a bloody Jew. I was called a Bedouin. And we were always being told to leave. Even if I went for a swim in the river, I would have little stones thrown at me by Polish boys. We were not welcome in our own town.

Of course, I didn't feel at home. We could have gone anywhere before the war, to Australia, to America, because we had enough money to buy a permit. But nobody was thinking of leaving.

It's God's fault. He said go forth and multiply. And then they multiplied, and there became three million Jewish people in Poland, and the anti-Semitism grew, and there were pogroms before the war. And the slogan went, 'Beat the Jews Up.' And they did.

Have I ever regretted being born Jewish? Not once — always. I still regret it. My friend, her father went to a shop, bought her a cross, put it on her neck, and said to her, 'Go.' He kicked her out. She went to Kraków. She survived and her family didn't, all because she was wearing a cross. Doesn't that make you think?

I am angry at God. If he let 1.5 million innocent children be killed, how can you believe? When Yom Kippur (the Jewish Day of Atonement) comes, I am devastated, I break down, because that day was sacred. I was brought up in a five-room apartment, and in the corner was my father standing in his *kittel* (prayer robe), and one by one on Yom Kippur he would give us a blessing. That's how I remember my father.

I was brought up in a Jewish family with all the traditions. No, I couldn't take up another religion. It's built-in. But that has nothing to do with believing. My mother brainwashed us that God is up there, so we imagined that there is a big armchair and God sits there. Now they are thinking of going to Mars, and they still can't find God on that chair.

I stopped believing because I have that image; I can't get rid of it: my father was dying in the gas chamber. I have the image that he said *'Shema Yisrael'* (praying 'Hear O Israel') and that haunts me. It kills me. God was death. He was not listening.

I didn't think I was lucky to survive. The loss was too colossal. It was meaningless to be free. Nothing could make me happy, because I went to hell. I had no interest whatsoever in anything.

I was glad when I met my husband that I found someone.

I didn't want to be alone. He was very good-looking, and I was a poor orphan. But we were not a good couple. He was a fantastic, good man, never said a rude word. I could never find a connection with my husband, yet he was working very hard as a tailor. We had nothing in common.

I couldn't talk about things with my husband. He was worse. He went to such shocking places, seven camps. He told me some things. He wouldn't do even a testimony for Spielberg; it was too terrible.

And I didn't talk to the children about the Holocaust. They found out themselves, because I didn't want to put the burden on them. But they are still saying that they are second-generation Holocaust survivors, and that makes me very sad. They are suffering. They have no relatives, no uncles; at the holidays, there was no grandfather.

When my twins were born, it was a shocking time for me. I had no one left in Poland, no sister, no aunty, no cousin. My husband had to work. He left at eight o'clock in the morning and worked twelve hours. I knew nothing about children. I just thought I will keep them clean and give them food and then I will send them to school.

I was so unsure of myself. I could have crossed into Germany illegally at night. But how could I go with two little kids? So we stayed, and the communists took over Poland, confiscated our passports. My life was five years or six under Hitler, and then under Stalin. It wasn't a good picture.

I was a good mother physically. I couldn't give them knowledge, but I gave them a roof over their heads and food on their plates. Emotionally? There was not much hugging. And I feel guilty — a lot. Maybe I was withdrawn. I loved the kids, and they are very good. Maybe I didn't do so badly, because they are absolutely good to me, and caring.

Being in Poland after the war was terrible. People were being arrested, and my husband liked to talk politics, and I was always scared that they would come to get him.

On the way to Australia, we stayed in Israel for two months. There, I had my loving brother, my loving family, and my friends from school and from camps. They were all nice to me. We came by plane from Warsaw, and in Budapest at the airport two Russians with rifles took away our papers. I started to panic. I said, 'Oh, not again; they are back.' But they gave us back our papers.

When we were flying from there over Israel, suddenly we saw the plane was full of Jews who took out their *tallits* (prayer shawls) and started to pray. I will never forget that. I said, 'Is that possible? Jews praying like that? Free?' I hadn't seen a *tallit* in years.

And then we landed in Israel and I saw a policeman — a Jewish policeman in a Jewish country. I couldn't believe it. My brother picked us up in Tel Aviv, and he said he had a place for us. And I told him we were going to Australia. He was crying.

I was homesick later for Israel. Why? Every Friday night, my father would raise the wine cup and say, 'Next year in Jerusalem.' And then came the day when they said, 'You don't need to say that, you can go to Jerusalem any time you want.'

So many times I felt guilty that I should have stayed there. I didn't want to at the time because Israel was a very hard life and my brother in Sydney said there were plenty of jobs here. But I was dreadfully lonely in Australia. I didn't speak English. I didn't know what's what.

I went to the movies and meetings and holidays. But I was

always sad. I just kept going, but the past was always there, day and night. I live with it. I sleep with it. I wake up with it. There is no escape.

I see everything: how my family and hundreds of other Jews were packed into cattle wagons — it was standing room only. How long the journey took, I don't know. And you see them pushed out; they have to get out in Auschwitz.

Some survivors coped better than me. I would look at them. They were happy. They were dancing. Maybe in their hearts they were feeling it, but they were not showing sadness.

I seem happy? Maybe I am a good actress. When I would go to the Jewish museum here in Sydney, my throat would get tight. I would have liked to have been a guide, but I was too emotional.

What happened to me was bad. I was humiliated, I was beaten up, and I can't get rid of it. We were seventy girls from one city, we had to make two rows, and the Germans were walking and we had to pull up our skirts, we had to show them our bums. Whoever had enough fat went to work. Whoever was a skeleton went to Auschwitz.

I have been carrying this heavy weight with me my whole life, and the older I am it's getting worse. It was a colossal loss of family and of your young years. Teenage years never come back. I survived because I was young and the German men had to fight in the war and they had to have slaves to work in their factories. I live with that. And nothing can change it.

After seventeen, my life turned upside down. So how can you live and be happy? There's a saying, 'As you grow older, you get colder.' I will be healed when the earth covers me.

Eddie and Flore Jaku

BORN: Abraham Jakubowicz
14 April 1920
Leipzig, Germany

BORN: Flore Molho
28 September 1923
Thessalonica, Greece

After decades of conscious and careful avoidance, the past has become Eddie Jaku's present. He talks about it regularly, to school children and military officers, to diplomats, tourists, and German-speaking students, to never-ending roomfuls of strangers whose interest in his personal history seems to strengthen as he ages.

Thousands have listened to his story of survival, which he details multiple times a week at the Sydney Jewish Museum, something he has been doing through much of his long retirement. He has spoken, too, to a multitude of community groups around the country and sixteen times to military officers and cadets in Canberra, a decades-long endeavour that contributed to his Order of Australia Medal.

At an age where the voices of his contemporaries have softened, he has become a masterful raconteur. His delivery is warm and easy as he stands steadily before his audience, his voice skilfully building to a crescendo as he recounts his unlikely tale, which began in 1933 when he was thirteen and thrown out of his German school for being Jewish.

In need of an education, he was whisked away by his father to a boarding school, and spent the remainder of his childhood assuming the identity of a non-Jewish student, Walter Schleif, who had less to fear from Hitler's appointment as German chancellor than a Jewish boy from Leipzig.

Although he was busy learning the finer points of precision engineering, he was lonely being away from his parents, his younger sister, Johanna, and his extended family. So in November 1938, five-and-a-half years after becoming exiled in his own country, he boarded a train home for the first time to surprise his parents on their twentieth wedding anniversary. In the sheltered environment of the boarding school, where he was assumed to be an orphan, he had learned little about the increasing hatred being shown towards Jews in Germany, and when he finally arrived home he was surprised to find no one there.

History would remember this night as *Kristallnacht*, the infamous and frightening 'night of broken glass', and, in anticipation of the mooted pogroms that would devastate Jewish communities in Germany, Austria, and parts of Czechoslovakia that night and the following, his parents and sister had gone into hiding. But he had no inkling of this as he went to bed, alone in the apartment, to be awoken at five a.m. by the frightening din of the family's front door being broken down by German police.

He was taken from his room and beaten, saw his family dog being killed, and was then sent to the Buchenwald concentration camp. He languished there for months until an old boarding-school friend, now working as a camp guard, arranged for him to be released briefly into his father's care before he was to be taken to work, in exchange, as a factory toolmaker.

Instead, his father drove him to the border, where a smuggler took them both to Belgium. His few weeks of safety there ended with his arrest by Belgian police for being German. In the ensuing months, he was interned multiple times, for being German or not, depending on the progress of the war and his location. Eventually, he made his way back to Brussels, hid in an attic, was denounced, and by November 1942 had been transported to Auschwitz.

He spent more than two years there, forever on the precipice of death. He faced the daily risk of being hanged if the air-pressure units he was servicing at a Bayer medicine factory failed. He saw his father being trucked away to the gas chamber. And he lived with the constant fear of being gassed, too, in his barracks if an outbreak of lice was detected.

His brutal time in Auschwitz concluded just as brutally in January 1945, with a three-day death march and then a harrowing train ride back to Buchenwald. There, he broke his self-imposed rule to never volunteer, and put his hand up to be a toolmaker at a German factory. In return, he was chained to a machine from six p.m. to six a.m. every night for the first bitter months of 1945.

In the final stages of the war, the factory was closed down, its forced labourers left to sleep in a forest with no food and under dwindling supervision. After several nights, he escaped by hiding in a pipe, and later in a cave, existing on slugs and snails for weeks until June 1945 when, desperately ill and weighing twenty-eight kilograms, he finally encountered US troops. His war was over — one month after the end of World War II in Europe.

His story is long and distressing, and he waited until the 1970s to relate it publicly. Since then, he has told it regularly, week after week, verbatim and voluntarily. But beyond his smooth delivery, there is a personal sense of urgency. As much as he is among the last survivors, he knows that his audience is the last generation of listeners, and more than anything this compels him, in his late nineties, to keep speaking.

Not so his wife, Flore, who knows his story well. Over a long marriage, she has come to understand her husband's tale of survival, with all its intricacies, as intimately as her own story. She is also a survivor. But where her husband has opted for oratory, her choice has mostly been silence.

Born to a Jewish family in Greece, she spoke French and Ladino, the now mostly dormant language from Spanish Jewry. When she was seven, her family moved to Brussels, where her father ran a laundry agency and her mother was a dressmaker.

When Germany invaded Belgium in May 1940, she was working at a local council, and, while bans were soon imposed on everything from the playing of American music to the freedom to walk the streets at night, in some ways her life continued as ever. She still went to work and lived at home until 1942, when she was ordered to appear at the local Gestapo headquarters, informed that she had been denounced by a colleague, and told she could no longer work at the council. Soon after, she was presented with a long list of items — fork and knife, blanket — to assemble, and told to appear with them on 4 August 1942 at a former military barracks in Malines, between Antwerp and Brussels, before being deported.

In the intervening days, her council boss learned of her intended fate and instead arranged through the Belgian Resistance for her to be taken to France where she would assume a false identity.

For the next two years, she lived in Paris, known to everyone but her brother and sister-in-law, with whom she shared an apartment, as Christiane Delacroix (Christine of the Cross), the most non-Jewish name she could contrive. For all that time, she abandoned her own religion, attending church instead, and with a French identity card she obtained rations and avoided starving.

When Paris was liberated in August 1944, she joined the enormous crowd cheering General Charles de Gaulle at the victory parade along the Champs-Élysées. Within weeks, she was back in Brussels, living in her old home, and, soon after, working in her old job.

Within months, she met her future husband, but their paths to marriage were markedly different. Both Jewish and based in Brussels, they had endured very different wars. His had been spent largely in concentration camps, his identity reduced to a number, and he had emerged emaciated, gravely ill, and having lost all of his family, bar his sister. She had assumed the identity of a Frenchwoman, had lived in an apartment in another country, and no one in her immediate family had been killed. By her own admission, she had done nothing to survive and he had done everything.

They married in Brussels on 20 April 1946 — Hitler's birthday, as they both point out — and, with the first of their two children, they arrived in Australia in July 1950. Their union would be unlikely but enduring, spanning two continents and more than seventy years.

Eddie

I don't think I had so much joy at liberation. Once you know nearly all your family is dead, you realise that life is miserable. Liberation is freedom, but freedom for what? To be alone? To have to say *Kaddish* for other people? That's no life. I know many people who took their own life in Germany when we were liberated.

Many times, I was very sad. But I had to learn to live again. And the most important thing was to be nice to your friends. Kurt Hirschfeld and I had been in a camp in southern France with 4,000 Germans. We became very good friends. Before I was deported, he came to my home in Brussels many times. He didn't have any family then. His parents had already been killed in Berlin.

Until I got married, he was the most important person in my life. Brothers wouldn't be as close as us; he understood everything. We were together in Belgium when we were in hiding and we met again in Auschwitz.

Kurt was in block 38 and I was in block 14. I had to walk twenty-five minutes in the rain and snow to get to him. He kept me going. When I was in hospital with jaundice, he risked his life to bring me soup. When we were on the death march, he couldn't walk any longer and I hid him in an attic.

I knew if he had survived, he would go back to Belgium.

I found him in a little Jewish canteen for soldiers in Brussels. They thought we would never let go of one another. I think we stayed there for ten or fifteen minutes, both crying, looking into each other's eyes. It was something fantastic. Kurt found a girlfriend before me. He married in February 1946 and later moved to Israel, and I married in April.

Did I need a wife? No. I needed a mum. I was very lonely. I missed my mum and my life, even today, and Flore replaced her. Kurt showed me the letters I wrote to him after we got married. And I said many times I had found a new family. Her mum, she accepted me with all her heart. So I got a wife and a mum.

I was a very difficult person when I married. I didn't want to go dancing, I didn't want to go to the cinema, I didn't want to go anywhere where there were a lot of people. You had to avoid crowds because that's where you would be detected; somebody could recognise you. I had been programmed to look out for danger. My wife didn't know anything about this. People didn't realise how bad it was and how easily you can lose life.

When I was back living in Belgium, one day I got a message that the Germans had returned some of our photos and documents. It was a big box of things: my German passport; different identity cards; a book where my father had started paying insurance for me; a work book from when I graduated as Walter Schleif; an identity card from my mum, from my dad, everything.

It was very, very emotional. I cried. My sister, she wouldn't even look at it, she was too upset. In your subconscious, you close something; you can't bring them back. You realise your parents and your valuables and everything you loved has gone. And suddenly it comes in front of you. It's a shock. For a long time, I put it away and didn't want to look at it. It was a long time after I was married that I took it out of the drawer.

The good things that happened were so few that you couldn't compare with the bad things that happened to you. People generally are good, but I remember cruelty more.

I haven't got trust in people like I had before. I tell you how unfair life can be. We had been a group of four men in Auschwitz, with a lot of Hungarians there, many were elderly people, and it was bitterly cold. They were standing near a fire, and our *kapo* (prisoner in charge of other inmates), a Jew from Austria who had sent his own uncle to the gas chamber because he had done something wrong, came and took down all their numbers because they had stopped working to warm themselves up. Just to put their names on the list was a death sentence; they would get seven lashes on their backs. I had had seven lashes. I had survived, but I knew they wouldn't survive. And I said to him, 'Put my name down instead.' He said, 'All the time you want to be a volunteer. I have to bring names.' They all got seven lashes. I never saw them again.

In 1945, four of the survivors, we saw that *kapo* in Belgium. We wanted to do something, make an affidavit, put him in jail. We went to the police and we wanted to get him arrested. But it was just after the war, and he had influence: he had a girlfriend, a minister's daughter, and he was going around with two German Shepherds. The police warned us if we didn't stop, they would deport us back to Germany.

I am still outraged by this. There is a man who had killed people indirectly. Let him be judged in a court of law. And we couldn't do anything against him. You don't have to do that; you volunteer to be a *kapo*. If you denounce someone, you must be punished. I am not saying you must be killed, but this man had to go to jail. It makes me feel that there is no justice. I think that very strongly.

In Belgium, I didn't feel comfortable, because they denounced me to the Germans. They are the enemies — and they denounced me, the refugee. That really hurt. Eventually, I felt all right there, but I never felt safe. After the war, I felt there were people who said Hitler didn't do a good enough job. When I started working in factories there, it felt like they were uncomfortable I was there, that I had taken a job from a Belgian. I felt comfortable in Australia. Many times, I heard people saying 'reffo', but I didn't take any notice.

At first, I spoke very little about the war. People asked me; I have a number on my arm, so I can't forget. But voluntarily for thirty years, I didn't want to speak about it, because it contradicted my feelings about creating a family as normal as possible.

I speak now so that people are aware of what's happening, how people can be so cruel. Talking, it lifts the burden, but it's hard because you get emotional. Sometimes, I have to stop and have a drink of water.

I call the audience 'my new young friends', even the officers at the Defence Force Academy. I speak to thousands of people. These are thousands of people who say, 'I will help you, that this will never happen again.' Maybe they won't do it straightaway, but when they get older maybe their children will follow up what I said.

I believe that I make a great impact. We were at a dinner, there were about 150 people. Two women came up to me and said, 'Are you Eddie Jaku? You spoke at our daughters' school ten years ago.' So there it is, children who heard me speak years ago are still talking about it.

I hope my story will stay in their hearts. And it stays. They remember that moment. Like yesterday: I had a school from the Blue Mountains, sixty people, and thirty-two women tourists from all over, and they came into the museum and listened. I said, 'I cannot forgive or forget.' But in the same sentence I say, I don't hate the Germans, because I believe hate is a disease. And one woman said, 'What would you like them to do so that you don't despise them anymore?' I said, 'They can't do anything.'

Before I leave, I am concerned that I leave a message, because Germany was the most educated country. My grandmother lost a husband and two sons fighting for Germany in World War I. They were my people. That was my country. And suddenly people of that calibre became murderers.

Even in Buchenwald, thousands of Jewish German men in this tent, we got our bread, and suddenly I felt sick, I had to run to the toilet. I left my bread there, I swear to you, twenty minutes later my bread was still there. This was German upbringing.

I believed in Germany as a beautiful country. I don't hate them, but I don't like them. They can send me anything and give me as much money as they want, but I will never forget or forgive.

I was invited a few years ago to be on a TV show about forgiveness. I am glad I didn't go because they would have asked me for forgiveness. And who are the other people on this panel? Some people whose child was run over, or someone's husband has a girlfriend and she finds out and she forgives him. How can you compare this to what happened to us, to the murders that they have done?

Do you know that I am invited every two years to go to Germany to visit my proper home? Every time, I answer very politely: 'For personal reasons, I cannot go.' When I was in hospital for three months after the war, I kept asking about my chances. I found out through a nurse that the doctor gave me a thirty-five per cent chance of living. So I made a vow; I said to my God, 'If you help me to come out alive from this hospital, I promise you I will never set foot again on German soil.' And I never did.

My God? I was brought up religious, but I am not religious. I don't believe in God anymore. If there is a God, it would be a God for everyone and this would never have happened. If there was such a power, he would instruct his wise men to make everybody the same. Because it says in the Bible if you do good you get rewarded and if you do bad you get punished. I didn't see any punishment for the people who have done so bad.

Flore

Before the war, my only contact with Jews was my family. Everybody else I knew was non-Jewish. I was completely assimilated. After the war, I felt intensely Jewish. I went from one extreme to the other.

After liberation, I could shout that I was a Jewess. It really brought me close to my people. I only was mixing with Jewish young people then. I hated all the others who had done that to us.

When I went back to Brussels from Paris, this friend said to me, 'Do you know there is a Jewish canteen for soldiers?' I couldn't believe it. I was in awe: a Jewish soldier! And they asked for Jewish girls to come and serve on their day off. There was dancing as well. One day I was in that canteen, there was a group of men there, and they pointed out one of them. He had just come back from a concentration camp, so everybody jumped on him: 'Did you see this one, that one?' That's how I met Kurt.

When I was in the office one day, Kurt comes in with this other guy. When I knew some Jewish survivors were coming in for ration cards, I used to jump at the counter. I wanted to look after them. I felt so much pity for all of them.

So I went to the counter, and that's when Kurt introduced his friend Eddie, and I said, 'What are you going to do now?' I couldn't care less what he was going to do now, but I wanted them to know that I cared about them. He said, 'I am going to Australia.' He could almost not speak French. He said, 'Are you coming?' I said, 'Why not?' as a joke. I went into the office and said, 'What do you know, one of the prisoners asked me to go to Australia.' They all thought it was so hilarious. I didn't have any need to go to Australia.

After that, he wanted me to visit him, to come over for a meal. I thought I would offend him if I refused. He represented nothing of my upbringing, of my background. I always thought, as a joke, I will marry a poet, an intellectual. My brother came to Brussels to meet him and said, 'He seems a nice boy.' If my brother approved, for me that was good enough.

We are both survivors. I didn't understand that for a long time because I never really felt the persecution. I was terribly lucky. No one in my immediate family died. My father was not taken. My mother was not taken. When the law came that said we had to put on the shop window that we were a Jewish business, or that we had to wear the yellow star, we got the yellow star, but the Greek Jews decided not to wear it. I didn't realise how serious it was: in Brussels, I was still going out after eight o'clock at night, after curfew.

I lived normally in Paris. It didn't bother me having another identity; I was always Flore. With my French identity papers, I could get rations. I did the shopping and cooking and cleaning. I went to the theatre. I was not unhappy. That's why I felt always embarrassed — because I didn't suffer.

I often think how lucky I have been all along, without doing anything. I was never in an attic. I was never hungry. I never did anything to be able to survive.

And yet it seems I am more angry than my husband about

what they have done to my people. When I came back after the war, a woman came to see me. The council used to give money to the wives of Belgian prisoners of war, and a colleague had fallen in love with one of the wives, who was working there part-time. They told me after the war that the colleague thought that if he denounced me then they would take my job away and the woman would be able to work full-time. So he denounced me. He went to prison later, and his own wife came and begged me to interfere, which I didn't; I am not the pardoning kind.

I find what they have done so humiliating. Although I enjoy things and I can appreciate beauty, I am more on the pessimistic side since the war. They destroyed all the descendants of all those people that they killed. They deprived the world of so much. I always say that if I had been in a camp, I wouldn't have died from lack of food or extreme work. I would have died of vexation.

The Holocaust was a defining moment in Eddie's life, not in mine. That was for him a big, big happening in his life. Not for me. For me, it's in the totality of it. I feel on my shoulders the pain of the Jews. I feel more than Eddie, I reckon.

I loved Australia from the start. When I saw shops closed in Sydney for a Jewish holiday, I thought we were in heaven. Who would even mention that you were Jewish in Belgium?

I felt very Jewish but not in a way that involved God. In the beginning in Sydney, we really kept away from religion, but not on purpose; it just didn't come into our lives. We didn't belong to a synagogue. We didn't go even for the high holidays. Our son Michael had a bar mitzvah at fourteen. I don't know if we would have even made him one, but when he reached thirteen, and other boys were having theirs, he said, 'Mum, I want to make my bar mitzvah.' I was very pleased.

We worked very hard, and we moved eight times — Eddie is the typical wandering Jew. He would take a year to convince me to move. Then a week after we moved, he would lose interest. He doesn't take roots.

I never went to hear him speak. It embarrasses me. It bothers me when he talks about the Holocaust. For me, it's personal. I remember years ago finding it was a bit too much, Eddie always speaking of that. We went to a celebration, and Eddie would speak of the camps. And I would knock him under the table. I suffered for the people who had to listen to him. I thought they thought, here he goes again. In general, people don't like to hear of tragedies. They want to hear of happy things. Me, I don't want to share.

Eddie is like a star. People stop him at the shopping centre. They must have come to the Jewish museum and he spoke to them. They are very, very touched by Eddie, not, I think, by the Holocaust. Only his face remains, not the tragedy. The kids are emotional for what happened to Eddie. And when they say, 'I will never forget you,' they mean Eddie. But I think of the masses of people that were killed.

Even when they praise Eddie, I am sure that at that moment they mean it, but it will not live with them. I know that we have to teach the world — although for me, it's for nothing. In terms of accepting Jews, it will not make a difference.

I don't like the commercial side of the Holocaust. But there is one very good thing. Talking makes my husband rich. It gives him almost a reason to live. It's incredible. I bless the museum every minute, and I bless Eddie.

Jack Greene

BORN: Jacob Grünschlag
29 May 1925
Bolechów, Poland (now Bolekhiv, Ukraine)

He is a convivial man, generous with this time, and straightforward in a manner that seems at odds with the many identities that have brought him, late in life, to this cosy lounge room at the other end of the world.

He was born Jacob Grünschlag, the middle of three sons of a Polish timber merchant and his homemaker wife, a placid young man who liked to laugh. This is who he was in his formative years, with a German-sounding name that took him to a local Jewish primary school and on to a neighbouring high school with plans, when he graduated, of joining his father in business.

For most of his life, he has been Jack Greene, a name that belies his European origins and which he adopted in another era in another hemisphere. In this guise, he has been a Sydney accountant, a father of two and grandfather of four, a donor to charities, and an unstinting storyteller, the man who was able to inform the author Daniel Mendelsohn about some of his murdered relatives in his book *The Lost*.

But he is also a product of his past, and although it is the best part of a century since he last sat at a table with his parents and his two brothers discussing politics and life in Poland, he still reflexively turns his head to the sound of 'Yankel', the enduring nickname from his childhood.

In his nineties, he is one of the few surviving Jews who lived before World War II in Bolechów, a comfortable town of timber mills and tanneries and a vibrant Jewish life. Up to 4,000 members of Bolechów's 12,000 pre-war population were Jewish. At war's end, apart from those who had survived in Russia, forty-nine were alive. Today, by his own estimates, he is, at most, one among six.

His story of displacement began well before Germany invaded Poland in September 1939. For as long as he could remember, he had had a lingering sense of being a stranger in his birthplace, a sentiment that was reinforced as he played in the street with neighbourhood children and they reminded him, as teams were chosen, that he was Jewish, not Polish, as though the two groups were inherently separate.

He was fourteen when World War II began, and his latter childhood became a steady erosion of liberty under successive intruders. First to arrive in town were the Russians, and then for varying periods came Ukrainians, Hungarian, and Slovak soldiers, and finally the Gestapo. He never saw fighting in Bolechów, but, as the restrictions imposed on Jews increased, he often wondered if he would return to a free society.

In October 1941, his mother and older brother, Gedale, were caught by the Gestapo in a round-up of Jews. He saw neither of them again. He spent days hiding with his father and his younger brother, Bumek, in a hayloft and then in a stable as the captures continued and he lost twenty-five of his cousins, his four aunts, and his grandmother. No other Jewish student from his school year survived.

Within a year, Bolechów was considered to be free of Jews. The only members remaining in the community were labouring for essential German industries as he, his father, and brother were at a nearby sawmill. But even that protection soon ended. In August 1943, having escaped imminent death several times with the help of a local Nazi, the three surviving Grünschlag men escaped to a forest. For the next year, with the help of a Ukrainian peasant, they lived in an isolated bunker, 1.2-metres high and 3.5-metres wide, a tiny squalid space that they shared with eight others.

The months that followed were once inconceivable: tight, cold, deprived. Several of those hiding in the bunker, starving through a freezing winter, died there.

By early-August 1944, the Russians had liberated Bolechów, and, like that, he and his father and brother walked back into their old town. They returned to their home, minus a mother and eldest brother and any possessions they had once claimed, and tried to resume living as a newly configured family unit. But the nightmare had not quite ended; he was drafted into the Russian army, and deserted it. In danger of being killed, he fled back to Poland – losing contact, in the process, with his father and brother, who had left for Munich, and eventually Australia.

So he departed Poland alone and permanently, crossing into Austria and then Italy, where, at a displaced-persons camp in 1945, he met his future wife, Sarah. They married in Palestine in May 1947.

In the early 1950s, at his father's urging, he and Sarah prepared to emigrate from Israel to Australia so that the remnants of his family could be reunited. Twelve days before their flight, however, his father sent word that they should not come; he was moving to the US, and then to Germany.

Their preparations all but complete, the couple left for Australia anyway, arriving in Sydney in April 1951.

When we were liberated, our home in Bolechów was vacant. We stayed there, and a young Jewish Russian officer came in and started to talk to me. He asked what happened to the family, and I told him my mother and brother were killed in October 1941 and a friendly Ukrainian dobbed them in.

My father wasn't happy that I talked to him. He was reluctant to stir up something — they might take revenge; you never know. After three or four weeks, the Russians came and threw me into prison. At midnight, they called me out for an interview. They read what I had told Greenberg, the Russian officer, and then they asked me what I knew at the time the Soviets withdrew from Bolechów and the Germans came. By two o'clock in the morning they said, 'You can go home.' It was dangerous — there was a curfew — but I had no choice.

I wasn't scared — among the Russians, you didn't fear for your life; but again, you do what you are told, you have no say — although it left a bad feeling. But it didn't stop me from speaking. I felt I had to get it out of my system. So then I talked to whomever I could. Maybe it was a release, I don't know. My brother Bob (Bumek) bottled it for years, and it punished him. But I was very happy to talk from the word go. It was like any other subject.

It's decades since they killed my mother and my brother Gedale. I never thought I would last ten years after that because you thought such bad things would affect your health and your drive to live.

Being liberated is the start of your problems, not the end. It's a whole life in front of you. You have to start to create life for yourself. Then I thought, well, I've got seven years, ten years, enjoy it. You survived. Live. Enjoy life.

When I got on the train to leave Poland, I travelled for four weeks on the roofs of carriages, and I felt I would go wherever I like, I have life in front of me. I know eventually I will have to be trapped and work. But right now, I am free. It was immense joy.

I came to Italy in July 1945 and met there an ex-employee of my father, Manes. He said, 'Look here, I haven't got anyone, you haven't got anyone, let's be a family.' It was a very good feeling, that someone cared, someone liked your company, your presence. I met his future wife in Poland, and I travelled with her all the way to Israel, and we also became very good friends. When she died, there was a phone call from their daughter. She said, 'Now tell me, you must have been related.' And I said, no, we were not.

He was like family. The bond was so close that people thought, oh they must be related. If I had some problems and wanted to discuss something, Manes was there. He talked. He cared. I could have gone to America to be with my uncle and aunt after Italy, but I knew Manes would love me to join him in Israel, so I thought, well, you're family; I will go to Israel.

Then because of my father, I had to go to Australia. I didn't dare to tell Manes. I remember Sarah and me circled for three or four hours around his house to tell him we were going to

Sydney, but didn't; I wrote to him from here. I felt I was letting him down terribly. He was very good to me; he wanted to bring me to Israel, and I deserted him. I still regret that.

When we came to Australia in 1951, you could get a job anywhere. My cousin arranged me a job as a packer at a wholesaler of crockery and cigarettes. I could speak Hebrew, Polish, German, and Yiddish, but not English. I'd had two lessons; I knew the word 'umbrella'.

Once I learned English, I enrolled in a night course in a technical college. After four years, I became an accountant, and within two years I started my own business. It's not a great story. It's a story of you-have-to.

Around 1960, I became Jack Greene. My son went to school and they couldn't pronounce his name. He hated it, and I didn't like it, either. To start with, it was a German name. It was difficult to pronounce. I am still Jacob officially, but they told me at the time, 'There's no such name as Jack. Someone called Jacob is also called Jack.' But now Jack is a name. I made it Greene with an 'e' at the end so I would be different. In the business, it was easier to pronounce Greene. But there are more Greenes than people. I should have picked a nicer name.

I do believe in God, in an upper justice. That's what lets you live or drives you to want to live, otherwise what's the point? Sometimes, you feel terribly let down; my mother was killed. Or after a killing of 1,000 people you say, 'Where is God?' The answer is you stop thinking about it and then you start believing in it a little bit, till the next disappointment. You hold on because otherwise there is no hope in life, there is no justice. You have to believe in something. Otherwise you just exist.

The main lesson I learned in the Holocaust is to value your

life. There's nothing more dear or more expensive than life. And I think if you appreciate it, you talk about it, you enjoy it. To survive was just impossible. What chance have you got? None, none. And then you survive. I had to pinch myself whether I am really alive.

Sarah was sad about it. She couldn't laugh like I laughed. I always liked laughing, funny stories, or memories from good times. I always enjoyed life.

I wanted to live, and there's a good German saying, 'to live and let live'. And there's another good Jewish saying, 'instead of being an angry fool, be a placid fool'. So to be able to live, you have to be a placid person.

After the war, I wanted to join a gang that would take revenge on the Germans. I thought of it quite a bit. And then, luckily, I thought I would be wasting my first years of freedom and I wouldn't achieve much. I hate them, sure, but I try not to think about them. To hell with them.

I realised it won't do me good; if I will be angry, I will suffer. But I think it's not the philosophy; I think it's the make-up of the person that gives you that feeling. It's a part of your personality.

My father was not like that. He felt let down completely by the world. And he left us; he went back to Germany and decided not to be in contact with us because he thought we were trying to scheme against him.

Two years before he died, he came back to Australia. We spent quite a bit of time talking then. I said, 'Listen, there was a period, ten years, where we didn't know where you were. What happened when you lived in Munich?' And he said, 'Don't you remember? I was on the train travelling with two big suitcases and two Gestapo men boarded and they found me.'

That was in 1978. That was thirty-odd years after liberation, and I knew he wasn't well. He had lost everything and he just couldn't recover. My father was a self-made man. Then no one had time for him. And somehow, he was derailed.

I come from a *shtetl* (small Jewish town) where my grandmother, my mother's mother, had three living sisters two kilometres away. My father had brothers and sisters. It was a very close-knit family. It meant a lot. During the Holocaust, everything disappeared. The family shrank all the time. Then you felt you were on your own.

Now what it means to me is my children and grandchildren, that's all. My only regret is I didn't have more children. I was a coward. I was afraid I wouldn't be able to support them. Because that's all you have.

The dearest are the grandchildren. To me they are everything. I cried the first time in the last fifty years when my granddaughters left for London. That's the only time I cried. I am sad about the past, but I don't cry about it.

I went back to Poland in 1996. My brother wanted very much to go, because he didn't remember that much, and so did two of his friends. My son went with us, and he loved it. I went because of my brother. And possibly there was some curiosity in me. Without them pushing me, I wouldn't have gone for anything.

I felt lousy, didn't like it for a minute. They saw the place. I saw in front of me the place where the Jewish town was, bit by bit. Every place: he was killed here, that Gestapo man was there, and so on. It was like a punishment.

The houses were there, but the people weren't there. You didn't know anyone. I felt sick about the bad-doers, but not about all the people, because many were neutral, many were good. People in general are good. I think the war made me softer; give a person a chance if you can, or be nice to him to make him more comfortable.

I was happiest after the state of Israel was created in 1948 and I got a good job there, and then I would say the last twenty, thirty years in Australia. We used to go every year overseas, many times to Hawaii, take a beautiful apartment for two months. The saying was in Bolechów, 'like God lives in France'. And that's how I felt. We lived like God in France.

I treasure most my life and my relation with the family. I achieved a certain financial security that allowed me to do it. Australia provided me the means for it. We enjoyed it to the fullest. And that was worthwhile, everything. My friends who perished in Bolechów, they died in misery and that was all. We achieved a lot in this respect.

My life out of ten? I would say between seven and eight. Human nature is good — you forget the bad times; you remember the good times.

Kuba Enoch

BORN: Jakob Enoch

3 May 1926

Kraków, Poland

History reshaped Kuba Enoch's formative years in a way he could never have imagined, robbing him of one family and bestowing upon him two more.

Growing up as an observant Jew in Poland, he was the elder of two brothers, a city boy who loved scouts and who had not yet contemplated a possible profession when war intervened and he had no control over the remainder of his childhood, let alone his future.

He turned thirteen in mid-1939, and marked his Jewish entry to manhood with a bar mitzvah surrounded by his extended family. Within months, the celebration had become more than just a figurative end to his boyhood. In September, Germany invaded Poland, and almost immediately his teen years became a series of degradations, progressively more dire and unimaginable. As a Jew, he was banned from school. He was forced into a ghetto. One by one, his relatives were deported to concentration camps, their names added to lists of the condemned whose screams haunted the ghetto on too many nights. By the time he was eighteen, he was alone.

His war story is marked by solitude and by enduring friendships, and spans multiple camps. When the Kraków ghetto was liquidated, and his younger brother, Ziggy, was killed, he was enslaved for a year at the nearby Płaszów concentration camp, with its crazed commandant Amon Göth, depicted in the movie *Schindler's List*, and its constant executions.

He was eighteen when the unforgettable stench of cremated bodies marked his arrival at Birkenau. There, he was stripped, deloused, and crudely tattooed with a number on his forearm that, for a long time, would replace his name. By then, his mother was dead of typhoid and starvation, and he had no idea what had become of his father.

He was sent next to Buna (Auschwitz III), and toiled each day at an enormous industrial estate that supplied Germany with rubber and fuel. On Sundays, before receiving a daily ration of bread, he and other inmates had to run naked before SS officers, and those deemed unfit were sent to Birkenau to be gassed.

By the bitter opening of 1945, Russians troops were nearing the area, and he was forced to march for three days and nights towards Germany, before being loaded onto a cattle train to Buchenwald. By the time he arrived, two-thirds of the men who had set out from Buna with him were dead.

After forcibly clearing rubble from bombings and mass burying bodies, his enslavement finally ended on 11 April 1945, when US troops liberated Buchenwald, and thousands of emaciated souls staggered back towards life.

A month later, he joined a trainload of young men, among them the future Nobel Laureate Elie Wiesel, who had been granted a temporary home in Switzerland. (Wiesel and others were subsequently sent to France.) During his three years in Switzerland, he learned that his father had survived.

In 1948, he and forty-four of those young men, who would

become known as the Buchenwald Boys, sailed into Melbourne. He was one of only five to continue to Sydney, where he would eventually create his own family, spanning four generations.

Apart from a few images rescued from Polish archives, he has no photographs of his pre-war relatives.

On the train to Switzerland, I felt safe because we had the Americans escorting us with guns. We were protected suddenly. We thought we were top of the world.

We stopped once. It was the beginning of May, cherry time, and the boys hadn't seen cherries for such a long time. They jumped off the train and ran for some. Instead of picking them, they broke whole branches.

So a bloody farmer came running with sticks to hit us. The American soldiers tried to protect us, but then a rabbi who was with us, he said, 'You know, boys, you did the wrong thing, even according to Jewish law, because you destroyed things. You could take as many cherries as you wanted, but you shouldn't break the trees.' That's how they tried to bring us back into civilisation.

We were a rough lot. In camp, if you saw something lying there, it was yours. If I wanted to take it, it was there, I'll take it. If somebody died, he didn't need his shoes or clothes, you just took it.

I wanted to stick with the boys. That's the only people I knew. But we were completely green. We wanted to know how we were going to make a living. How would we exist, connect to society? How to learn, what to learn? In Switzerland, they tried to bring us back to a normal life. They tried to educate us — how to use a fork and knife, how to eat at a table, don't grab things. If you were invited to people's homes, they told you, do this and this. You had to understand you had different laws you had to obey.

I had to learn table manners. In camp, you didn't call it 'stealing', you called it 'organising'. You organised to get yourself more food. Now you didn't have to hide food anymore. You had to realise that there was enough. Switzerland gave me a bit of order and discipline. I was very happy there. That was the first time we met girls.

I think coming to Australia was my best move. It was all excitement. It was adventure; Europe to us was a cemetery. The first time we saw fruit when we stopped in Fremantle, we couldn't believe our eyes — fruit I had never seen in Poland, beautiful mangoes, custard apples. God created something unbelievable.

There was one girl on the ship with all the boys, and she was also from Auschwitz. She was my future wife's cousin. I met Kitty about a month later. We married in April 1951. Our first child was born two years after.

That was my dream, to establish a family, to have somebody to belong to. After 1943, I was always on my own. When you survive, you survive on your own, not anybody else. I tried to be a very good parent. I tried never to hit my children. I tried to talk to them. I think my children are very good. I am very proud of them.

My father loved the children very much. But he started to dominate me. I just couldn't take it. He thought I was still a little boy, a child like I used to be before the war. But I had been independent for such a long time, looking after myself.

The first time I talked about the Holocaust with my children was when they had to do school projects, so I had to talk to them. But I didn't want them to grow up with complexes. I spoke to my wife, of course. But nobody can understand. I used to have dreams, and she used to push me in bed, 'Wake up, you've got a nightmare, always running, running, chasing.' I didn't realise. She woke me up because I was screaming.

I spoke to two psychologists; I was trying to get reparations from Germany and I had to. It didn't help. The first one said, 'Why do you want money from Germany? How will that help you?' I said, 'How is that your business?' So I left him. I went to the other one. He said: 'As a matter of fact, I just came from a conference about the Holocaust in Spain, and I can warn you that when you get older it will get worse.' I said, 'Thank you, doctor.' I left him, too.

If I had a problem, I used to go to the boys from Buchenwald. They were part of my family. I had nobody else. If they had problems, they used to come to me. We would stick together.

They announced in Buchenwald that 11 April will be our rebirth, and the boys adopted it. Not only us — Frenchman, Dutchmen, all prisoners, Norwegian. You were reborn on that day. You're a new person.

Every year on 11 April, they have a Buchenwald Ball in Melbourne. I am not a drinker, but some of the boys are. My son was astounded how they could drink. They drank and danced. More than anything, they brought their wives, their children and grandchildren, all the family.

A survivor, not from Buchenwald, said to me, 'What have you got to dance about? Celebrate but don't dance. Why have a big ball?' It's not a question of dancing. It's a birthday.

If we didn't go to Melbourne celebrating, then my wife used to make a Buchenwald celebration here in Sydney on 11 April. We had a nice dinner at home and discussed how life goes on.

I am looking back on all my other friends and how they buggered their lives up because of the Holocaust. I have got a lot of friends who became very negative. One had six locks on his front door. He was such a nervous wreck; I don't know how he brought up his children. Some married out because they wanted to cut off from Jewishness completely. Some didn't have children, because they didn't want them to have the same *tzures* (trouble) they had.

My poor friends — not the boys — they have no continuity; they never created anything. Even if you lost everyone, your name could have continued. I think I'm winning the war because I created a beautiful family and I am continuing Jewish life.

I wear a *kippah* (skullcap) because you are supposed to, I don't know. I am trying to succeed to be an example to my children and grandchildren. You've got to live by example.

I believe because I have got to believe. I am part of the club — the Jewish club. You can't join a club and make your own rules. If you take away the religion, what have you got left? What do you believe in? Jewish food?

I would say eighty per cent of Holocaust survivors do not believe in God, because they claim no God could accept Auschwitz, or he must have been asleep. I have no answer to tell them otherwise. Even rabbis can't explain the Holocaust going with God.

But I read a book, *When Bad Things Happen to Good People*, and there you've got an answer to God that somehow I managed to accept. If God gave you a brain then you conduct yourself with your brains. You can't blame God for everything that happens. He created the world. A lot of things that happen in the world are because bad people created bad things.

There is good people and bad people. When I was working near Buchenwald, this German woman with a baby used to come through and she used to leave bread rolls under the stones on the side of the road for me — until the SS man saw her one day and he told her off. We went back to that town after liberation to get food. We hadn't seen milk for donkey's years. There was a place with a big queue, and local people were lining up. We just walked into the shop and got the bottle of milk, and as I came out I saw that woman standing there with her children, so I went back in and got milk for her. She must have remembered me because she thanked me so much. I returned the good deed.

People under normal circumstances can be very good and some are bad. But don't start asking me about people in camp. In camp, people exist for themselves. It was a question of survival. Some behaved very badly.

For me, Buchenwald was one of the better camps. It was a controlled environment where there was no actual destruction. People were dying of hunger and disease, but they were not dying by execution. I think you become used to everything eventually.

I went back to Buchenwald for the fiftieth anniversary of liberation. Everybody who came got a medal. The Germans gave me a medal — there you are. They put up beautiful tents with chandeliers hanging and food and music, unbelievable. My wife thought it was fantastic, so why shouldn't I appreciate it?

Rabbi Herschel Schacter, who went with us to Switzerland, was there. He organised a prayer service, and we prayed at Buchenwald. I thought it was the most stunning moment, the rejuvenation of the Jewish people. Hitler would have *plutzed* (exploded) if he knew Jews were praying there.

When I retired, I went with my wife on a bus tour through Eastern Europe. I noticed we were going to Auschwitz. I said, 'Darling, I've already been there; I'm not interested.' But she really wanted to go, so we went. It was astounding; it was a museum. It wasn't the same place. I was very upset. I didn't know what to make of it. I was completely lost.

After I went with my wife, I went back with my two daughters. It was much better this time. I was the master of my own destiny. I hired a taxi driver; he spoke perfect English. We were coming back from Auschwitz, and my daughters were crying. And I said to them, 'All right, have a cry and forget about it. Don't get too sad for me, please.' And one said to the other, 'How could this happen in Poland?' And this bastard taxi driver started shouting, 'How dare you? I will get you out of the taxi straightaway. It's nothing to do with Polish people.' I was a bit astounded at his outcry.

I never wanted revenge. I found revenge is self-destructive; it won't achieve anything for me. Number one, I was a little boy; I had no *koyach* (strength). Who could I take revenge against? I was no hero. I was shitting myself.

A lot of people don't buy German cars. I don't care. I can buy German goods. But I don't like to be associated with Germans, because I don't know what crimes they committed.

I avoid association. My poor wife, she couldn't understand why I wouldn't go to barbecues for years. Here, we were invited a lot of times. I just couldn't stand it. It was the smell of the crematorium when I came to Birkenau. It came back to me, this burning meat. Everybody hung around the barbecue. I stayed inside.

We used to be invited to parties. They would have a buffet and I would wait till everybody had eaten. I would never push myself first. My wife would say, 'Kuba, why don't you go and eat?' Because I had been in camp waiting for food. I don't have to do that anymore. I am in a country with enough food. Why should I fight for it?

I only cry when I have a memorial for my mother or for my brother. Tears come to my eyes. My biggest regret is the loss of them. And not having a picture of my brother. I would give anything for a picture of my brother. I remember him very faintly. All I remember is he was more clever than me.

Marianne Van Der Poorten

BORN: Marianne Stokvis

2 April 1914

Amsterdam, Netherlands

So much about survival is unexpected. Luck is prominent in many stories, and comes with endless variables. But through all of life's permutations, few could have imagined that Marianne Van Der Poorten, Holocaust survivor, would be sipping cocktails at 102.

A vibrant centenarian with a passion for celebrating, she marked a century of life with a brunch for 120 people. At 101, she was still living independently. At 102, after enduring an operation for a broken hip, she was back attending evening social events within weeks.

Her enjoyment of the present, however, follows a traumatic past. The daughter of a Dutch diamond merchant, her passage to early adulthood was mostly comfortable, with no hint of the terror that would spread so rapidly soon after her married life began.

She had grown up in Amsterdam, a keen basketballer and tennis player, and had met her future husband at a rowing club in the late 1930s. David Van Der Poorten was a doctor, eight years her senior. Their wedding photo from April 1939 shows a joyous couple on the steps of an Amsterdam synagogue, oblivious to the devastating world events that would chase their union. Within months of their marriage, Hitler had invaded Poland. Sixteen days after their daughter Malieke was born in April 1940, the Netherlands was attacked by Germany.

The progress of war made no allowances for a new family as restrictions began to curtail the lives of all Jews, even those who felt more attached to their Dutch nationality than to their religion. Forced to live under curfew, they were issued with identity cards bearing a large J, and were prohibited from buying food until after three p.m., by which time there was little if anything available.

As the war restricted their world and their future, it arrived, literally, at the young family's front door one day in the form of two Jewish friends fleeing the Gestapo. With nowhere else to go, they spent several weeks hiding in the Van Der Poorten home, which was also to become a site of Resistance work. Its park-side frontage removed the possibility of nosy neighbours, and, at night, Resistance members would arrive to falsify identity cards.

As deportations increased, David's vital position as a doctor gave his family some protection initially. He continued to treat patients, but now only Jews, thanks to ever-tightening rules. Sometimes, he ascribed them fake illnesses, and, with Marianne, concocted mixtures that made them seem ill, to delay their removal to work camps.

In this perilous time, and the rush to save countless souls, some things were impervious to war, however; in 1942, the couple's second child, Alfred, was born.

But there was little time to appreciate the joys of childhood. With Jewish lives increasingly endangered, by May 1943 the couple faced an enormous decision: how best to save their two small children. Their conclusion was to hide them – and in the process to let someone else parent them. So, relying completely on the goodness of others, with the help of a trusted neighbour they handed over their infant son and their three-year-old daughter to separate foster carers, and spent the remainder of the war pretending to be childless.

Before long, they, too, went into hiding, taking refuge on the outskirts of Amsterdam in the home of a woman David had known for much of his life. Before his marriage, she had been the caretaker of his apartment building. For several weeks, they hid in one of her bedrooms and were later joined by Marianne's parents, who had been hiding elsewhere in Amsterdam but who, at the woman's insistence, had also moved into her home.

Her hospitality, however, was not selfless. Through visiting friends, Marianne and her husband learned that the woman had been speaking openly about harbouring Jews. Realising that she was jeopardising their lives, they made plans through the Resistance to move elsewhere. As a courtesy, David told the woman that they were preparing to leave. But before they could, she tipped off German authorities, who were then paying informants for details on those attempting to evade capture.

Interrogated by the Gestapo, the couple were imprisoned for two nights and then taken by train to a camp at Westerbork, where they arrived on 18 April 1944. It was their fifth wedding anniversary. Within a month, Marianne's parents had been taken to Auschwitz, where they died, and, by September, Marianne and her husband were interned at Theresienstadt, where he worked as a doctor and at night she volunteered to tend to other people's children.

In June 1945, months after liberation, she was finally reunited with her daughter and son. Six years later, having given birth to a third child, she came to Australia with her family.

In the years since, she has been widowed and divorced, and her two eldest children have died.

When the war ended, my husband was very ill. Lots of people came to Theresienstadt from Auschwitz, and they brought with them typhus, and he caught it. He spent six weeks in hospital.

The children were still with their foster parents then. I was lucky because my late daughter was hidden by my neighbour's sister. They wanted to have a child, so I knew she would be safe there. And my son went to friends of my neighbours.

It was too dangerous for them to be together. What could I do? They were not safe with me, so I had to hope that my children would be all right with other people, and I was nearly sure they were.

I was always thinking about them. In the meantime, I looked after other children in Theresienstadt. I helped at night to feed them and take them to bed. One of them came to Theresienstadt as 'Alfred Van Der Poorten', which was my son's name, with a question mark against his name on the list. My husband was sure it was our son, Alfred, who was only a baby the last time we had seen him. It wasn't him. But I said to my husband, 'It doesn't matter; we will still look after him.' And then I saw a girl who looked like my daughter, and after the war we took her back to Amsterdam, too. I didn't have a home then, but I found people who didn't have children who would love to have that boy. And the girl went back to the people who had hidden her. So for that I didn't have any worries.

I hadn't seen my own children for three years. They didn't remember me when I went to get them. My son was a baby, and my daughter was only three when she went to her foster mother, Nan. She was very fond of her. My daughter didn't want to come back to me. Whenever I combed her hair later, for a long time she said, 'Nan never did that.'

It was very difficult for her to come back and see that I was her mother. And it was difficult for us. We were always compared to the foster parents, for quite some time. It was a little bit troubling. I just tried to be as good a parent as possible.

Our other daughter was born in 1947. I wanted to have one child born after the war because I had missed all those years with my children, so I wanted one child from the beginning.

I loved Holland. I wanted to stay. It was the place where I was born; I grew up there, and went to school. But my husband was afraid that the Russians would come to the West. He wanted to go as far away as possible.

It was quite hard leaving. But anyway, we came here, and it was quite nice. And I had here an aunt and uncle and a few friends, and we were very lucky that we had a large house that belonged to a doctor, so after my husband studied again he could have his practice there. In the meantime, to earn some money, I had a boarding house.

I tried, especially because of the children, to live a normal life. First of all — never cry when they are there. There were times I was crying in the war when my friends disappeared. After my parents were taken away, I didn't cry anymore.

And never bother them with our experience, because even

now my daughter knows people whose parents had been in concentration camps, and they pester their children with it, and we never did that.

I didn't like to talk about the war. I wanted to forget. Lots of children were always reminded that their parents had been in a camp or went through terrible things. And we never told them anything. We thought, why should we bother them? Why should they have a bad life? It was already terrible that I had to remember. So why should they? I think it was the right thing, yes.

I always thought it was important to enjoy things. I have always celebrated birthdays. I go out on Sundays with my daughter-in-law for lunch. I have a strawberry daiquiri or a Campari with orange. We go away to Terrigal every school holidays — four generations: me and my daughter, three granddaughters, and seven great-grandchildren. I love it.

I have survived and I have lived — both. I sometimes thought about revenge. The Germans were top of the list. Three years after the war, I was driving and I saw on a bike the lady who had betrayed us. Later, they gave her twenty years in prison, but they freed her already after three years. Of course, I hated her. I told my husband, 'There she goes.' I wanted to drive over her. If my husband hadn't been there, I would have done it.

There's a lot of people who are not too good. My experience was that. We were hidden with people, and they betrayed us. There are good people and bad people, and maybe, unfortunately, there are more bad people than good people.

Sam Gelber

BORN: Shloma Gelber

1 May 1925

Düsseldorf, Germany

Details can be a changing commodity in Sam Gelber's inimitable life. Some vary because of history: his date of birth, the liberal transliterations of his given name (Shloma/Szloma/Schloma). Others, he recites meticulously: the arrival of German troops in his town, the death of his father, shot by a policemen as he tried to reach his only son inside a Polish ghetto.

There is a proud, defiant tone of success to his story but also an air of survival that endures so long after the war officially ended. Born in Düsseldorf, he left Germany with his parents and younger sister when he was six or seven, as the ascent of Hitler portended a difficult life for Jews, and his grandparents urged the young family to join them in the comparative safety of Poland.

They arrived in Częstochowa in the early 1930s. He attended a Jewish primary school and then a trade school. His father was a fruit wholesaler. He spoke Polish and Yiddish at home.

At fourteen, before he had even had time to contemplate a livelihood, his life was upended. Almost as soon as the war had started, German soldiers were in his town, an arrival that his father initially welcomed; he took his only son to the train station to meet the troops, and, after conversing with them in German and being plied with chocolates and cigarettes, he returned home reassured that the invasion was not a bad thing.

That sense of comfort, however, was shattered within hours. The next day, Jews were forced from their homes, told to run, and then shot at. Some of those who survived were taken through the city to an army camp. Within weeks, his mother and sister had been sent to Treblinka.

The only family life he had known was over, and, with Jewish students banned from attending school, so was his formal education. He and his father were forced into a ghetto, and when that was liquidated, they were among 900 people, mostly men, transferred to a nearby plant producing ammunition, arms, and wood-distilled gas generators. From there, his father was loaded onto another truck, and he never saw him alive again. By 1941, aged sixteen, he was alone. He has been responsible for himself ever since.

For the rest of the war, he was part of an ever-dwindling demographic, avoiding multiple atrocities when so many others did not. From the main ghetto, he was moved into a smaller ghetto, before it, too, was liquidated in 1943, and some of the few remaining inhabitants were taken to the local Jewish cemetery and shot.

He was among just 4,000 survivors now, and like many he was sent to a nearby forced-labour camp, surrounded by electrified wire. There, his life depended on reconditioning ammunition for the very war effort that had already murdered his family.

His war was long but never far. Working in a kitchen at one time, sometimes making bullets, burying people at another time, he was whipped and kicked on multiple occasions and forced to live on meagre quantities of food. In six years of misery, however, he was never more than a few kilometres from home.

Then, in January 1945, he heard shooting and a gate crashing. Russian soldiers had arrived at the labour camp and so had liberation. He walked back into Częstochowa, and returned to freedom without his family, with no clear idea of how to live an adult life.

But even his homecoming was short-lived. Within months, he was conscripted to the Polish army. Later, he moved to a displaced-persons camp in Austria, smuggling goods across the border to Czechoslovakia and illegally changing money, whatever he could do to generate an income before arriving in Australia, stateless, in 1951.

When he talks about those years now, he is animated and shows neither sadness nor tears. But mostly his history has been carefully guarded. He has spoken little of his past, sometimes talking to his late wife and his children but rarely in great detail. One of the few times he varied from that pattern was in 1995, when he spent almost three hours recording his war experiences with Spielberg's Shoah Foundation. Even then, he was reluctant to talk, and only did so at the urging of his late wife.

I have two birthdays. I think I was born in Düsseldorf in 1925, but when I went into a camp I was only fourteen, and I made myself four years older. They would have killed me otherwise; I was a child and not useful.

My second birthday is 5 August 1921 — in my passport, everything. And I couldn't reverse it. I went to a big solicitor here and we couldn't change it for any money. You have to get a birth certificate, which I haven't got.

My father was a translator in Treblinka. He ran away from there and came back to Częstochowa to find me. He tried to get into the ghetto, and a Polish policeman shot him. Nobody came to me when he died; everybody looked after himself, for his own life. I was still a child; I didn't know what to do. I did nothing. I lived in the ghetto and went to work every day. I don't know what happened to him after. I suppose they buried him somewhere.

No one survived, except one cousin. She is in Cherry Hill, New Jersey.

It was hard when we were liberated. I had to make a living by myself. I had to get a pair of socks, a shirt, anything. I had no feelings. In the evening, I saw some vodka, so I went and took two cases and traded it with the Russians. Was it stealing?

I didn't feel anything. I didn't mind at all. Everybody was taking everything for free. People went into the shop — it was empty — and took things.

I lived day by day. No rules at all. It wasn't easy, but I made it. I don't remember being lonely; I always had a lot of friends. I am more lonely now than I was then.

In the Polish army, I made a lot of money. In the beginning, they gave me a rifle and I thought I would have to stay on duty and train. But I didn't do anything. I never had to fire a shot. I never went on duty. I was sitting in coffee houses and restaurants. I had bags of German Marks because I sold army supplies. I had that much money I didn't know what to do with it. Even though I had lost my parents, I felt for the first time happy. It was the best time in my life.

One day, there was a pup, and this Russian railway man said, 'Would you like to buy a dog?' And I liked the dog so much, the look of it. The head was crooked; it hit me straightaway, it was a lovely dog. You couldn't touch me. If I walked with him in the street and you touched me, he jumped. Such a beautiful dog.

I didn't like Europe; I wanted to get out. I applied everywhere: Argentina, Canada, America. And my first papers came in from the Australian consulate to go for an interview.

I came to Melbourne first. You couldn't see a car. You couldn't see a person. I said, 'What am I doing here?' Then I came to Sydney. I couldn't get a job — and I went to the consulate to go back to Austria. I didn't like Australia. There was nothing here. You couldn't get a piece of salami. You couldn't get a piece of cheese. Devon was the salami and Coon cheese was the cheese. There was nothing here, not a coffee lounge — you want a coffee, you went to the milk bar: 'You want white or black?' No restaurants. Six o'clock, the pubs closed. It was very cheap everything, but I couldn't get a job.

I was lucky I didn't go back. They wanted a guarantee that I wouldn't be on the government's expense in Austria. And I said, 'I haven't got anybody,' and they said, 'I am sorry; there is nothing we can do for you.' After, I was working three jobs in Sydney — and then I felt better. I got money and I saved. Then I had key money for a unit. Later on, I worked for twenty-eight years in real estate.

It was a fantastic decision to come here — not good. It's a very quiet, nice life. So long as you have nothing to do with the police, you can live like a king.

I do believe in God. I shouldn't — because I was a child in a camp, and he didn't help me at all; not only me, everybody. But I do believe in God. I am not religious. I believe somebody must be in heaven.

When I cry, I cry very softly. Sometimes, if it hits me, I cry about my wife. I don't remember if I ever cried about the war; maybe I did, but I don't remember.

What's to cry? It's done, finished. I really don't want to think back. But I had to tell my grandchildren, my children. I just spoke to the family. And I did an interview for Spielberg. My three granddaughters, after they saw it, they were crying all the time: 'Papa how did you get through this?' I had tears in my eyes. The most treasured thing in my life is my grandchildren. I don't want them to worry about it. So I said, 'Everything is over — no more problems.'

I used to be a guide at the Jewish museum. Then I heard a friend of mine talking to some children about his story, and I couldn't stand it. And the manager told me, 'I can see on your face it's very hard for you to do.' It was too much for me.

I wouldn't go and look at a film from a concentration camp; you remind yourself, oh, they did it to me, too. I don't like movies, number one. Since my wife passed away, I never went to a picture show, I never went to a theatre, I never went to dancing or these kinds of things. I didn't feel like doing it.

I had some very bad dreams. Somebody is running after me and shooting. I remember very well all the stories that happened. Sunday, they came in; and Monday, they threw everybody out of their houses, and the SS were lying on the road with machine guns, *puk, puk, puk*. We made it — me, my mother, my father and sister — we all made it at first, but then they separated us. It was very scary.

I don't talk about my parents now, but I see them in my dreams a lot. My sister would be in her nineties now. What a beautiful girl, a good ice-skater.

It's possible I didn't show love to my children. I didn't have anybody after I was sixteen; you think about yourself. I was much better with my grandchildren. I love them to death. I do love my children, but it's different with them. In my heart, I feel the grandchildren better than the children. That's how it is.

What sort of a father and husband? Maybe not so good. I was out all the time, always busy. Somebody rings me up Sunday morning, 'I want to see this and this', so I went; business before pleasure. I was a terrific salesman. When I retired, they begged me, 'Come over for two days a week and teach the new salesmen how to sell properties.'

I never went back to Poland. I wouldn't even look at it. I hate that country. They used to stand in front of the Jewish shops, the anti-Semites, and they used to sing, 'Our best advice is don't go into a Jewish shop, because they will rob you.'

I don't feel anything bad about Germans. A lot of people do. I don't want to speak German, but I don't hate the Germans. I hate the Germans from the war. I remind myself of all the things they did. Not the soldiers; I am talking about the police and the SS and the Gestapo. These people I hate. I hate the Poles, not the Germans, because a Polish policeman killed my father.

I am afraid of nobody. Nobody and nothing. What should I be afraid of? I didn't do harm to anybody.

Before I came to Australia, four of us went to the park. We were in Liegnitz, in Poland, on the grass, joking and drinking, and an old gypsy came to us. 'Would you like me to tell you your future?' I said no; I never believed in it. One said, 'Okay, tell me.' So then I said, 'Tell me my future, too.' Whatever she told came true, 100 per cent: I am going far away, I will be well off, I will get married and have children, my wife would go before me, I would have a long life. And she was right.

I didn't have a transition from childhood. I didn't have anything, no life at all. But after, I was never hungry. Never.

Hella Wilk

BORN: Chaja Rivka Weingott
21 August 1925
Łódź, Poland

Hella Wilk is sitting at her kitchen table, talking about the past with a mix of nostalgia and disapproval, when she rises mid-sentence. She is a small, forthright woman – 1.47 metres before age erased a few more centimetres – and she exits wordlessly, returning with a sturdy picture frame that seems oversized under her slight arm.

'I want to show you something,' she says, and carefully places the frame on the table. In it sits an old black-and-white photograph – not the original, which belonged to her late aunt, but a copy or perhaps a copy of a copy – of a family gathering from the late 1920s.

There are dozens of people in the picture: bearded old men and demur young women, a little girl looking sidewards, a man in a shirt and tie, another tilting his head up to be seen from the far end of the back row. At the front, a few children are on the ground, the girls with their feet politely to one side, while behind them the gathering expands, some adults seated, others standing in a haphazard arrangement of people assembled in another place at another time.

This was Hella Wilk's world and the people who filled it when she was growing up: her great-grandfather, her grandparents and parents, multiple aunts, uncles and cousins, and Hella herself in the summer of 1929 when a moment at her annual family gathering at a Polish holiday town was captured for posterity. More than thirty people are in the picture. She is one of only three who was still living after World War II.

'This one finished off in Stutthof from what I hear,' she says now as she begins an itemised account of her family's fate, pointing out one of her many aunts who died not of old age but prematurely in a concentration camp.

'That's my uncle,' she continues, indicating a man in one of the rear rows; he was offered a chance to escape the Łódź ghetto during World War II but refused to leave his sister. 'He could have survived,' she says, still dismayed all these years later. 'It was his choice.'

In her tenth decade, she is a woman of specific emotions. She speaks frankly and is not overly demonstrative. Yet her eyes well and her voice chokes frequently as she sits in this light-filled space on the other side of the world and remembers the last time she saw her parents and her sister. More than seventy years have passed since they were separated at Auschwitz and only she emerged alive, but the trauma of that separation remains sharper than almost any memory in her long life.

The Holocaust is her life's great marker, years of Nazi tyranny effectively severing the first part of her life from the many years that followed. In that opening chapter, she was the eldest of two daughters. With her sister, Dziunia, a voracious reader but deaf and mute, she belonged to a vast family that not only holidayed together but also sometimes lived in the same apartment complexes.

She grew up in Łódź, where her father was a wholesaler of horn buttons, but considered herself Jewish, never Polish, a sentiment reinforced as far back as she could remember by the anti-Semitic names thrown at her by neighbourhood children.

She was fourteen when World War II began. Germans troops arrived in Łódź within days, soon rendering her town a place where Jewish men were dragged from their homes and Jewish women had jewellery ripped off them in the street.

By December, she, her parents, and her sister were among the first families to move into the Łódź ghetto, squeezed into a two-room apartment that would soon house fourteen people, with no heating or electricity, a kitchen but no bathroom, and some clothes among the few items that were still hers.

The degradations amassed. Her education was stopped, restarting for a few months in the ghetto before being ended for good, and she began working in a leather-goods factory as winter's death toll mounted around her.

When the ghetto was liquidated, her father was working in its main office, and his position gave his family a temporary reprieve. They were among the last to leave there in August 1944, and were then forced onto a train that later brought them, her aunt and uncle, and two cousins, to Auschwitz.

She was nineteen when she arrived at the concentration camp, afraid and bewildered, and soon separated from her immediate family. She had seen her parents and sister for the last time.

With her cousins, she spent two days at Auschwitz, relieved not only of her possessions, but also of her clothes and her identifiable red hair. After two nights on a concrete floor, she was taken to a town in Saxony, where she spent much of the rest of the war working twelve-hour shifts at a metal press that was almost too tall for her to manage. Under the supervision of a sadistic SS official who favoured a whip and holding back on already meagre rations, she spent her days creating metal components for German anti-aircraft guns.

After eight months, in April 1945 she was taken to the Theresienstadt concentration camp, where she was reunited with a third cousin, and where, in early May, she was liberated.

In the weeks that followed, she learned that the Jewish Brigade of the British army was smuggling survivors to Palestine via southern Italy. She began the journey to Italy via Austria, but when she arrived in Salzburg she was told that the displaced-persons camp there was full and that the clandestine passage to Italy and onwards to Palestine had been suspended.

So she headed to a camp near Munich and stayed there for eighteen months. Then she waited in Paris for a ship to take her to Australia, where, sponsored by an aunt who had been living in Melbourne since 1913, she and her two surviving cousins arrived in early 1947.

With dreams of becoming a doctor, she worked instead in a factory sewing clothes. She married a fellow survivor from Lodz, who had spent the war in Russia, their union spanning more than fifty years, and they had one child. Decades after her own education was halted, her son graduated from medical school.

After the war, I put on a lot of weight. I didn't know about food. How could I? In the ghetto, we couldn't cook; if we got some potato peelings, that was something.

Later, I loved many foods, but they didn't agree with me. I loved sausages, I loved fancy food, and I loved fried food. I was renting a room in a boarding house in Melbourne, and I wasn't supposed to cook there, so I went to restaurants for more than a year. I had too much fried food because I liked it, but I wasn't used to it, I didn't know what it would do to me, and, by the time I realised, it was a bit late. At the age of twenty, I had an ulcer.

In Theresienstadt, when the war was over, we had enough food — they gave us a big bowl of soup and some barley — but we were always wondering if we did. After being hungry for so long, we overate; we didn't know how much was enough.

The Russians had walked into Theresienstadt one evening in May 1945 and said, 'Oh, you are free, we are liberating you.' And the next day was the end of the war. Yes, I was sort of happy. But then I got a list of survivors, and my father's name wasn't there, and it dawned on me that he was gone. I was sure that out of all of my family he would have survived. I don't know why — because I wanted him to. When it started dawning on me that he hadn't, I really got depressed. I have never been one for crying so much; I am not demonstrative. But if I do cry, it's about the Holocaust.

When we arrived in Auschwitz, we didn't know what was happening. I didn't know anything about this place. My sister was eleven, but she looked eight, and they said, 'Who is the mother of that child?' And my mother, who was sometimes absent-minded, quick as anything she said, 'I am.' So they pushed her to one side with my sister and pushed me to the other. I was trying to explain to my sister what was happening. She looked at me …

I was taken away, and my hair was shaved. Hair is very important. It's personality. To have your hair shaved, it was very demeaning. It robbed you of your identity and your humanity. We were unrecognisable. We looked inhuman.

When our hair was growing back, when they had already moved us to the factory, at least we looked human after a few months. We used to work twelve-hour days, and we walked a good half-hour there, and most of it was during winter. I remember I looked up once as we were walking, there were houses, and I saw a light in a window. It was a lamp, amber coloured, and it gave a warm, homey-glow. And suddenly, that brought up nostalgia in me. It was a reminder of some other time.

There was no point in me going back to Łódź after the war. I didn't want their reception and I didn't want Polish citizenship. I don't want to live in Poland. I don't give a damn.

I had wanted to leave Poland before the war. I didn't feel Polish at all because I was called names: 'sore-infested Jewess'. I remember I was three years old on holidays and a little girl said to me, 'I can't play with you; the Jews killed Jesus Christ.'

Where would she have heard this at three? All I ever heard was 'the Jews killed Jesus Christ', which of course they didn't. I never even knew Jesus was a Jew until the first day at high school when we had history and I opened the page of a book and they mentioned that.

I hated the anti-Semitism in Poland, and I hated the fact that I was a second-class citizen and I couldn't go to university. Soon enough, my aunt sent papers to come to Australia. We went from the DP camp to Paris, but the French Indochina war had started and the boat was requisitioned, so we had three months in Paris. That's when I really had the feeling of freedom.

Walking those wide boulevards and being on the street, looking at normal life — it still wasn't quite normal then, even in Paris — that really symbolised freedom.

On the way to Theresienstadt, they had made us walk through a town, and it was the first glimpse in so long of what we used to have: a normal street with beautiful shops full of beautiful clothes, burnished shiny shoes with beautiful polish. Every shop window had a portrait of Hitler, and there were huge banners outside everywhere with swastikas. They were flaunting their Nazism, the thing that degraded us and wanted to destroy us.

And here we were, bedraggled, tired after ten days, hungry, unwanted. We looked unkempt, and we felt it. And this huge hate welled up in me. It really made me realise what we missed, what normal life was: shops, streets you could walk on. We hadn't had a normal life for years and years. This was a shock.

I do get angry about injustice. Forgiveness? I am quite happy sometimes if people get their comeuppance. After liberation, I saw that the town had been ransacked — broken windows, everything boarded up, no signs of life. I felt some sort of relief; they deserved it.

It was hard getting used to life in Australia. There was another set of rules. I had to go to work. I was lonely although I met friends right away; all the newcomers gathered together. Other people, they didn't really ask too much about what had happened. They didn't really have an interest in understanding what it was to go through the war.

My aunt knew and didn't want to know. When her younger daughter came back from Queensland to do her Bachelor of Arts exams, of course I was quite jealous. There I was working at a factory, doing sewing at the machine — it was not quite the thing that I looked forward to. I hadn't finished high school, so I couldn't go and study. I was a bit bitter about that.

My aunt lived in a house with thirty-six steps to go up, a mansion. She really took care of the three of us. We had to go to the city to buy some clothes, because our skirts were too short, probably because of a shortage of material in Europe, and we stood out. On the way there, my aunt said to us not to talk in Polish. But what else could we speak, for goodness sake? I knew no English.

She sent us to a teacher who was very good in English grammar, but she didn't know how to teach foreigners. After two lessons, we said to aunty, 'This is hopeless.' So I read newspapers. And when I went to the doctor or the dentist for a check-up, the *Women's Weekly* and the *Woman's Day* were a wonderful way to learn English.

It took a while to get back to the way we had lived before the war, to the standards that I had grown up with. My husband and I started off in a boarding house, in one room, and that's why I didn't have a child for a long time. Coming from a middle-class family in Poland, I had a one-bedroom flat in Melbourne, and I didn't want to get stuck there all my life. So we waited to have a family. In the end, I didn't wait long enough, because our son was born while we still lived in the flat, and I became quite depressed.

The first compensation money from Germany helped me to get a house. My cousin wouldn't take it — not money from Germany — but I couldn't afford not to take it. It wasn't a matter of pride; it was a matter of need.

The Holocaust made me much more cynical. You can tell me something, and I will be always doubtful. I don't take anybody's word unless I have got evidence. All my life afterwards I am the one who stayed in the back.

Who remembers me from back then? My aunt died in 1984, and she hardly remembered me as a child. My two cousins have died. All my best friends are gone. The ones that are left, I cut my ties with them a few years ago. I don't see many.

The family is missing. You notice it everywhere. You see somebody has a sister and an aunt, a normal family, and you haven't got a sister, nobody close to you. All right, at my age not everybody could have an aunt or anybody still living. But even in younger times, I didn't have much family left.

I still have my son. He has a family. He knows about my past. He knows I lost my family. He knows I was in Auschwitz, and he did see the film *Schindler's List.* But I didn't talk to him about it as a child. I didn't want to remember it.

I never wanted to remember it. I was in Israel forty years ago, and I didn't go to Yad Vashem (the World Holocaust Remembrance Centre), and I am ashamed. Now I would go.

But I was frightened; I thought if I went there, I would just live the nightmare.

I didn't want to live with it. But it keeps encroaching. You see old films; every now and then, there is a film with Germans and wartime and I watch it. Why do I watch it? I don't know. I shouldn't watch it. I don't watch the Hitler ones. I don't want to see Hitler. I can't look at a swastika. For a while, I couldn't even listen to German. I didn't want to see their uniforms. I saw an American film six months ago, and there were still too many German uniforms and swastikas for me. I switched it off.

It was only six years of my life, but it keeps coming back somehow. I don't want to remember. But I just can't seem to forget.

Phillip Maisel

BORN: Falk Majzel

15 August 1922

Vilna, Poland (now Vilnius, Lithuania)

He knows 1,000 stories of survival: the elderly woman whose long life after the Holocaust was tinged with the guilt of having inadvertently sent her young niece to her death; the inmate temporarily released from Auschwitz so he could sell stolen diamonds for his Nazi captors; the Jewish woman who fell in love with her SS guard.

Phillip Maisel has heard more first-hand accounts of the Holocaust than almost anyone. Since 1992, he has been recording testimonies at Melbourne's Jewish Holocaust Centre as an ageing and willing witness to the horrors that stalk so many of his contemporaries.

In a quiet room with a big black screen and a professional set of lights, he chronicles the intimate details of other peoples' losses, mastering the intricacies of filming more skilfully than he has shielded himself from the legacy of listening to so much tragedy.

For decades, he has devoted four days a week of his long retirement to the painstaking recording of testimonies from those who, like him, outlived Hitler's plans. Largely self-taught, his dedication — he has been involved with 1,000 of the centre's 1,600 testimonies — has consumed more than a quarter of his long life, and has been recognised with an Order of Australia Medal.

But there is one story that will always stay with him. Shadowing his years of detailed documentation is his own tale of tragedy and survival, and the loss of most of his extended family, a history as harrowing as all the others, and one that belies the smile he wears today.

He was born in 1922 in Vilna, now the capital of Lithuania but then a Polish city with more than 100 synagogues and 200,000 residents, 55,000 of them Jewish. By the time he was twenty-three and the war was over, he would be among the tiny percentage of Jews from his hometown still alive.

He was one of three children, born within minutes of his twin sister, Bella, and six years after his brother, Joseph. Both his parents — his father, who was a flax wholesaler, and his mother, who died when he was ten — were from Russia. He was raised in a Russian-speaking kosher home, attended a Polish school, and was well versed in the laws of Judaism and in his city's changeable history.

Throughout his life, Vilna had known many masters. Once the capital of the Grand Duchy of Lithuania, it had come under Polish control in the early 1920s, was occupied by Soviet forces in September 1939, and by October that year had been transferred to Lithuania.

Under Soviet occupation, his life changed markedly. His family's assets were seized, and, having recently completed school, he went to work not at his father's business, which had been taken over, but at a paper shop, later becoming technical secretary of the local branch of the Soviet paper workers' union.

Life was different and difficult but still tolerable, and then the pace of World War II changed his hometown's fortunes again. By June 1941, the city was controlled by German forces, who quickly issued the first of many anti-Jewish decrees. Suddenly, Jews could not walk on the pavement of their own city. They had to wear a yellow star on their clothes to identify them. They were subject to a curfew and could only buy minimum quantities of food. Within weeks, they were being forcibly removed from their homes.

On 7 September 1941, his once unspectacular life was abruptly curtailed when he and his family were given twenty minutes to grab what they could before leaving their home forever and moving into the city's newly formed ghetto.

Here, in the poorest part of town, where perhaps 50,000 were crammed into an area constructed for 5,000, he would spend the next two years, labouring at first, then training in six months to become an auto electrician.

He became friendly with a group of young people who had started a resistance group within the ghetto, and collected light bulbs that might be converted into bombs. He also resumed his friendship with a former paper workers' unionist, the poet Hirsh Glik, who would become best known for writing '*Zog nit keynmol*' ('Never Say'), today known as the 'Partisan Song' and the unofficial anthem of Holocaust survivors.

In his early twenties, he was again forced to recalibrate his expectations of life in order to survive, with minimal food, cramped living quarters, and long days working at a garage. Then, after two years, the ghetto was liquidated, and in September 1943 he was sent to Estonia. He endured six hard-labour camps over the following year, before being shipped to the Stutthof concentration camp and then to Dautmergen, where prisoners were dying at an alarming rate.

By then, his life had been reduced to surviving in increments:

first living through the harrowing rollcall that started early each morning and could last for hours; once enduring a merciless beating for having hidden some dried onions; marching for kilometres each day through residential areas to work long hours as a mechanic for the German war effort; marching back to the camp at night; and hopefully still being alive the following morning.

In April 1945, he was taken on a death march through Germany, led by ageing guards who fled as Allied forces neared. He was liberated within weeks in a nondescript village, with no possessions, no home, and no clear idea of how to live as a free man. After so much misery, freedom arrived with little fanfare, and the double-edged realisation that he was among the few European Jews who had survived Nazism.

Within two months, he was working as an auto electrician for French troops occupying parts of Germany, and he learned that the majority of his relatives, including his father, had died – but his two siblings had not. His brother, Joseph, who had been studying in France, returned there after the war and died in the 1960s. His sister, Bella, joined him on a ship to Australia, where they arrived in 1949.

Now widowed, he has two children and three grandchildren, and speaks to his sister every day.

———

I was liberated on 27 April 1945 in Ostrach in Germany. The war is finished, and you find yourself abandoned in a little village. Because I didn't know what to do, I returned to Balingen, location of my concentration camp. And I went back to work a few kilometres away in the same garage in Frommern, with the same tools I had been forced to use for the Germans — but now as a free man for the French.

We were a group of twelve mechanics, all Jewish, and all liberated. We didn't have any papers. We were still dressed in our striped uniforms. It took about three days to walk to Balingen. I had to go ahead of the others because I kept walking in a zigzag. For so long, I had had to march in a straight line. Now I had the freedom of crossing from one side of the street to the other, so I did.

I stayed in Germany for another three-and-a-half years, living in this little town where I was now one of the privileged people because I wore a French military uniform. And the Germans were suddenly very friendly. They said they never knew the Nazis had been so cruel. Every morning, we had been walking on the main street, from the concentration camp to the same garage, for about eight months. My landlady's room, where I lived after the war, looked directly onto the street. And she claims she never saw anything. The hypocrisy!

I didn't feel fortunate after the war, just the opposite. Here I am alive. What happened to my family? What happened to my friends? What happened to the world that Hitler destroyed? It was exuberance at first, but then came the reflection, and that was extremely sad.

I didn't think about whether I should feel comfortable staying on in Germany. I only thought about how I could settle down, find the family, and re-establish my life.

When I found my sister, we spent a few days looking for my father. We didn't know that he had passed away. And then we met a fellow who had seen my father burned to death; for me, that is the most gruesome thing. He told us in great detail what had happened. Then he said, 'Look, I had two children, and I lost them. You lost your father. Could I adopt you?' We thanked him very much, but then we departed. Nobody could substitute for a father.

The moment I found my brother and sister, there was a certain aim in my life. That's where the start of the happiness was. When did I feel fortunate? After arriving in Australia, not straightaway, after settling down.

My uncle had come to Melbourne in 1924. He sent me a photo of himself, a gentleman in a beautiful suit with a bow tie, two daughters in white dresses, in front of what looked like a palace. I thought he must have been very prominent in Australia. He wasn't — the photograph was of the wedding of my cousin, and the beautiful building was a synagogue — but they all had very good hearts. With them, for the first time in a long time, I felt the warmth of a family.

But I still felt a stranger for a very, very long time in

Australia. When I spoke Polish with my friends on the bus or the tram, people looked at me, sometimes with some disgust. It was only when I married that I felt, yes, here I will start my life and build my future.

I was very conscious of propagating the Jewish nation, of not letting Hitler win the war. A baby for me was something sacred. Even the crying of a baby was a pleasure because it was my baby, and subconsciously because I had lost so many people. This was the nicest period in my life, when my wife brought our two children home.

There is a Jewish custom to name your children after people who have died. We didn't follow it. My parents died in tragic circumstances, and I didn't want to evoke the memory of a cruel past.

When the children were older, I talked to them about the war. But I talked to my wife, Miriam, very, very little about it. Her mother had lost most of her family during the Holocaust, and as a child in Melbourne she had been introduced to this fear of the trauma of it. When I met her, I felt that I shouldn't inflict on her the pain of my memories.

As much as I was involved with filming all the testimonies, Miriam couldn't stand the Holocaust. And she didn't understand it. She would leave the room when the television was showing a film about it. She hated hearing about it. It was such a traumatic experience, she wanted to avoid even listening to it. I understood and tried never to hurt her.

Between ourselves, survivors talked, but not with others. When I came to Australia and I started to talk to my uncle about what had happened to me, and I tried to make it not too traumatic, he said I was exaggerating. He just couldn't comprehend that something like this could happen. Most of my friends were survivors, and some things I knew were so traumatic I could only tell them. It was quite important that we talked to each other because other people didn't understand.

The Holocaust is incomprehensible. But after the war, I still thought it would be a new world, a just world. One of the biggest disappointments for me was that there was not only not enough justice, but that justice was perverted.

One day, soon after liberation, a Pole living in Balingen came to us and said he knew where our *Lagerführer* — the cruellest man I had ever met — was living with his girlfriend. During winter, when it had been very cold and people were very slowly going to work, he had had a fellow stand at the gate and pour a bucket of cold water on another prisoner, someone who could hardly walk. The fellow died on the spot. This was a camp with 2,000 prisoners and sixty people dying on average every day because of the conditions — and he's supervising this.

Now he was living twenty minutes walking distance away from us. So I went over there with my friends, we arrested him, and we brought him to the French commander, who said to us, 'I am quite sure you want to have a talk to him,' and left us in a room with him. All my friends started to kick him — we had picked up some boots along the way with nails in the soles so you wouldn't fall on the ice — and they kicked him until he was bleeding. I couldn't kick him. I felt this is not the right way to punish him. I just stood by and let them do it. I didn't say not to do it. Everybody has his own way to express his anger.

There is no punishment sufficient for what happened — this man died a national hero — and in practical terms, it can't be imposed. The only compensation is that I can try to teach about the Holocaust and try to make the new generation of people decent people.

I work in the Holocaust centre, where I support the Jewish tradition of remembering. I record memories. There are memories you have seen. There are memories you hear from other people. There are memories that you create yourself to fill in the gaps. History is about people and how they respond to events. We know that the events of the Holocaust happened. But you have to see about thirty testimonies to get the real picture.

The testimonies are gruesome, and when I interview I try to get detached. I went through similar things; it was part of the life in the concentration camp. But I pity the person who is suffering.

I hear so many things that, like everybody else, I select what I should remember. I try to protect myself quite consciously. When I am listening, I am a machine, recording. If somebody cries, I check how much of this crying I have to record, two seconds, three seconds, or five seconds. A few hours later, I suffer a little bit.

If you would know how much I have learned listening to other people: about attitudes to life, about justice, about ethics, about humanity. My conclusion is that in this world there are a lot of good people who are never rewarded for what they have done. And I think every good deed should be rewarded in some way.

In all those testimonies, I have seen more optimism than pessimism. Did it surprise me? Actually, it didn't. I believe in humanity. I am alive today because of the humanity of many people.

I am hiding, a Lithuanian soldier discovers me and he calls out, 'Nobody is here.' He saves my life. When I escape from the ghetto, a Polish person, a complete stranger, hides me and when I leave puts some food in my pocket.

I am in a concentration camp in Estonia, during a storm I escape and I go to an Estonian woman who feeds me and tells me, 'You can come anytime to my house and I will feed you.' I go back to the camp. The SS guard, instead of punishing me for escaping, hears about the Estonian woman and he allows me, every Thursday when he is on duty between eight and ten, to go out, and she feeds me.

Humanity is very important — the most important thing for me. I want to be a good human being, and I educate people that everybody is equal. Every so often, I do something for strangers, because strangers helped me.

When I saw the world after the Holocaust, it wasn't the way I expected it to be. It doesn't mean that I lost trust in humanity. I didn't. It was still underlying the way I judge the world. I met a lot of decent people. I am here because of the kindness of complete strangers.

Now you know why I smile. It has been a very good life, despite all the suffering. I have seen good and bad in humanity, but I still believe that people are good. I survived the Holocaust, and with my decency intact. Yes, I feel very fortunate.

Afterword

'Good morning. My name is Agnieszka. I will be your guide through the Nazi concentration camp Auschwitz. If you have a mobile phone, please put it onto flight mode. You can take photographs here, but you cannot make phone calls.'

It is a quiet Sunday morning in April 2017, close to a lifetime since those imprisoned at Nazi concentration camps were freed, and, as it does every day except for Christmas, New Year, and Easter Sunday, Auschwitz is welcoming visitors. The first tourists have driven into one of the paid car parks, and, at the four-star hotel opposite the main entrance, breakfast is being served.

Time does not change for genocide. Blossoms continue to bud each spring on the trees lining the road to the former concentration camp, imbuing this place with a gentle perfume that belies its history. At the train station, a billboard welcomes visitors to 'Auschwitz, city of peace', a valiant effort to recalibrate the popular image of a name now synonymous with terror.

Auschwitz, the twenty-first century's byword for genocide, has become a museum. A leading tourist destination, it has a website and an automated booking system. There are still people in its brick barracks and even in a gas chamber — two million visited in 2016 — but now they are tourists who come to peer inside and out, to see where so many ghosts linger.

Most days, they file past the piles of old canisters of the poisonous gas Zyklon B, past the display of seized Jewish prayer shawls and the shoe polish tins brought by those who were hopeful they might indeed be sent to work here. They use the public toilets that have been installed in some of the brick barracks where civilians-turned-prisoners, within living memory, were confined. And when their inspection is over, they are free to leave.

Many join tours like this one, led by a genial Polish woman highly educated in the horrors that occurred at almost every step, with a detailed knowledge of Hebrew and of Jewish history, and a keen understanding of the delicacy required to guide visitors through Europe's biggest cemetery.

On another day of the year, a date not marked in its official opening hours, Auschwitz is again closed to the public. On this spring day, when the promise of new life clings to the surrounding foliage, and clusters of yellow flowers appear on the once grassless earth, Auschwitz assumes a different air.

Since 1988, on a date originally intended to coincide with the anniversary of the Warsaw ghetto uprising, thousands of people have marched the three kilometres from Auschwitz to Birkenau in tribute to Holocaust victims. On this day, in this normally quiet place of reflection, the mood wavers between triumph and sorrow as upwards of 10,000 people from dozens of countries – Jewish students from Morocco and Panama; Christians from Germany, Switzerland, and Austria – gather in the disused space between the old barracks. Where emaciated prisoners were forced to line up for hours for rollcall, there is, on this day, an air of informality. The grey order of wartime is supplanted by the bright blue jackets of haphazardly gathered marchers chatting over kosher sandwiches. Young girls in of-the-minute sunglasses giggle incredulously when they encounter Jewish students from the furthest recesses of the globe. ('There are Jews in Australia? Cool.') Then a ram's horn is blasted over a loudspeaker, the same ceremonial sounding that has marked Jewish life for millennia, and the walk begins.

Twenty-nine Australian high school students join the march in 2017, mostly sixteen-year-olds from Sydney, Melbourne, Perth, and regional New South Wales, each wearing a wristband remembering a child who was killed in the Holocaust. Ida and Gita, Wolf, Babi – these old names from another world are attached to the young wrists of a new generation, twenty-first-century youth walking in silent procession, arms linked as they exit Auschwitz beneath its famous sign proclaiming that work would free those forced to be here.

Slowly, they make their way along residential streets, past a smattering of local onlookers, past a little boy staring out from his lounge-room window, his face in his hands. For almost three kilometres, they are quiet as they head, within this bright sea of marchers, around a corner and up and over a small bridge. Only when they glimpse the train track that ends inside Birkenau do they finally unlink arms, and then, wordlessly and unconsciously, wrap them around one another's shoulders.

On this journey, most delegations are accompanied by survivors from their own countries, ageing members of an ever-dwindling pool of eyewitnesses reluctantly returning to this place so that a younger generation might remember their histories. But distance has become keener with time, and this year, for the second successive year, there are no Australian survivors to provide a personal soundtrack to the journey of these young Australians. Instead, they travel through Poland with students from Florida, and the testimonies they hear are from those who have made a home in North America.

The voices of survivors are dimming. But their stories remain intensely personal on the grounds of orderly Auschwitz, which is unexpectedly diminutive, and all the way to Birkenau, eight times larger and now mostly a collection of preserved rubble and the shells of old buildings. More than one million people were murdered here. Many of their names are lost forever. But each of them was someone's child. They were Marianne Van Der Poorten's mother, Hella Wilk's little sister, Marianne Schwarz's father, and many of the people Rina Schuldiener ever loved.

History has inextricably linked Poland to the stories of so many survivors. It is the location of multiple death camps, and as a nation it witnessed enormous losses. Almost five million Poles died during World War II. Of the six million Jews killed in the Holocaust, three million – ninety per cent of a once thriving community – were from here. Half the people in this book were born elsewhere in Europe. But add those who were forcibly taken away or whose families were, and only one of the eighteen who survived had no personal connection to this land.

'They say it's not the best idea for a county to lie between Russia and Germany,' begins the recorded commentary on a hop-on, hop-off bus ride around the national capital, a phoenix-like metropolis whose recent past hovers only just below its extensively reconstructed exterior.

Warsaw was once a place of markets and squares and

nineteenth-century townhouses. But after the general uprising in 1944, the occupying Germans systematically razed the city. More than eighty-five per cent of the historic centre was destroyed, leaving behind, for those few residents who had avoided being exiled, a lunar-like landscape of almost utter devastation.

A coded map recounting that time shows a grid that is mostly grey, signifying the vast swathes of once gracious buildings, often centuries old, that no longer existed at the end of 1945. Sprinkled across the gloom are tiny patches of orange. In a city that would take years to reconstruct, these are the few buildings that were left standing at war's end.

One of them was Lena Goldstein's family home. An above-ground unit with a view to an internal courtyard, it outlasted the city's tumultuous past, as it continues to do, although it is no longer the comfortable place of her memories. An abandoned space within an old apartment block, it is locked up and weed-strewn, and cut off from its former neighbourhood by a newish major road.

Across town, the stranger's bathroom in which she cowered for eighteen months has also survived, an anonymous apartment block with its silent history as an unlikely haven. And the square beneath which she existed for half a year in a foetid space of air and dirt has been cleared of rubble, and, like so much of the capital's UNESCO-recognised historic centre, has been beautifully restored, with a shiny Starbucks outlet competing for attention with alternating neon signs for expensive watches. The modernist American and gracious Swiss embassies lie just metres away from this place that was once cut off from the world. Now the world gathers here to eat and shop and take in a city's unique history.

These days, Warsaw's chequered past emerges through its eclectic cityscape – from the long-abandoned buildings whose owners never returned to reclaim them to the towering Palace of Culture and Science, Stalin's mid-century socialist-realist skyscraper and the most visible legacy of the city's communist era.

Not all parts of Warsaw's history, however, are as obvious. The hop-on, hop-off bus tour comes with a free map, pointing out many local features: the royal castle, the old town. It also lists a kosher restaurant – a jarring acknowledgement of life for those who assume that Poland's long Jewish history ended in 1945.

Thirty per cent of Warsaw's pre-war residents were Jewish. They had shops and families, 400 synagogues, and nine daily newspapers, and they lived with varying degrees of religious observance in the cultural capital of the Jewish diaspora. But their collective voice was largely muted when so few survived World War II, and even further with the onset of communism.

On the drive through Warsaw's rebuilt streets today, past its verdant public parks and comfortable cafes, the two-hour-long bus commentary includes many references to the city's Jewish connections – its multiple synagogues and schools, the Jewish organisations based here – but they are invariably expressed in the past tense.

Death is a recurring theme for many searching for Poland's Jewish roots, even as the acclaimed POLIN Museum, a shiny new edifice documenting a millennium of Polish Jewry, celebrates that same community's life. The country's chief rabbi, Michael Schudrich, an American who moved here in 1990, spends as many of his working hours tending to life as he does to death; advising one day on the appropriate handling of bones that have just been unearthed near the Sobibór extermination camp, and on multiple occasions every day confronting the same seemingly impossible equation: how to maintain 1,400-odd Jewish cemeteries, built for a once vast community, when there are so few people remaining to tend to them.

Before the war, Poland was home to 3.3 million Jews. At its end, nine in ten were dead, and after liberation significant numbers of those still living fled elsewhere. For those who remained, many hid their religion because of its uncertain welcome in a communist world, or because they were worried about what a Jewish future might entail given what its recent past had provided. From 1945 to 1989, when communist rule ended, Poland's long Jewish culture, heritage, and history were rarely discussed in public.

There are still Jews in Poland – around 7,000, some say, and possibly thousands more, Schudrich believes, with many only just learning of their Jewish heritage. There are again synagogues with rabbis and congregants, philanthropic organisations, kosher restaurants, and openly observed festivals. In Warsaw, where there is a Jewish school and day-care centre, tourists clamour to see not just the beautifully resurrected old town, but the Nożyk Synagogue, the only pre-war Jewish prayer house still standing, and to seek out the few remaining sections of the once menacing wall that contained close to 500,000 people inside Europe's largest ghetto.

History has been erased in parts and preserved in others, but it still lingers. On the same week that twenty-nine Australian students march from Auschwitz to Birkenau, a man in a smart business suit walks down Warsaw's busy Nowy Świat Street, a restored stretch of old buildings and new cafes. He bears a proud demeanour, a confident gait, and what appears to be a yellow star on his lapel.

From a distance, it might be a paper flower. But up close, his yellow embellishment bears a striking similarity to the insignias that wartime Jews were forced to wear on these same streets, before being barred from them, and then removed from them entirely, as they were through much of Europe.

His dress is startling. Then a second person walks past wearing the same insignia, and then a third. A few metres beyond stand two women handing out paper daffodils to passers-by.

It is the seventy-fourth anniversary of the Warsaw ghetto uprising, and, across town, staff from the POLIN Museum are distributing free paper daffodils – a symbol of memory, hope, and respect. Inspired by one of the leaders of the uprising, who was himself anonymously sent a bunch of daffodils each year, the paper flowers, when opened, resemble a six-pointed star.

Not everyone who is proffered a yellow flower on this sunny day accepts it. But many do, and many of them are young people. That night, across multiple television stations, every newsreader dons the same yellow shape. So does the Polish president.

There is Jewish life in Poland, as in Europe. But it is different. In a city whose Jewish houses of worship were all but lost to genocide, there are again regular services at the Nożyk Synagogue, but the sermons are delivered in English or Hebrew or Polish, and not in Yiddish, the old language of eastern Jewry that for so long filtered through these streets.

A taste of that old world can still be found at the POLIN Museum, where audio guides are available in many languages, including Hebrew and Yiddish, and in the in-house restaurant that purposefully serves dishes now rarely seen outside of private Ashkenazi Jewish homes: *cholent* and *kreplach* and *tsimmes*.

It is an intentional reminder of a world that has all but gone, a backwards glimmer that can be seen, too, in Kraków's old Jewish quarter, Kazimierz, a once thriving Jewish neighbourhood where the future cosmetics giant Helena Rubinstein was born to a local family, just beyond the spot where a newish restaurant called Babelstein stands today. Only 4,000 of Kraków's 69,000 Jewish residents survived the war. And in the decades that followed, the Kazimierz area, once a centre of life, was neglected and mostly avoided. With so many of its former inhabitants gone, it became an empty, unsavoury place, only revived after Steven Spielberg's Holocaust film *Schindler's List* was released in the early 1990s, and curious visitors began trooping through the area to inspect its locations.

Now Kazimierz has been revived as an old Jewish neighbourhood. Its central square is still lined with several synagogues, one of which has been converted into a museum, and with restaurants called Ariel and Rubinstein, where spruiking staff members stand out the front, menus in hand, to entice visitors inside. They offer chicken soup and 'Jewish caviar' (chopped chicken livers), and host bands playing the joyful klezmer music so beloved of this district a generation or two ago. Mostly, though, these restaurants are neither Jewish-owned nor kosher.

'The musicians are Polish,' says our cheery walking tour

guide, Ania, an effusive and knowledgeable local who spent five years immersed in Jewish studies, as she leads us around the busy square. 'That's why we sometimes call this place Polish Disneyland.'

An hour away from Auschwitz, Jewish life is being reborn in Kraków, but not as it was when Kuba Enoch lived here. The city now hosts a popular annual Jewish culture festival, and every night the songs that once filled Jewish theatres are played to a new kind of audience: mostly inquiring strangers keen to dip into the city and its culture for a few days before flying off somewhere else.

They wander through the restored narrow streets, take in the charming atmosphere and the rich history, and then sometimes stop for a meal at an inviting cafe whose detailed interior has been carefully furnished to resemble the inside of an old Jewish tailor's shop. On the menu there are luscious cakes, warming soups are graciously served from individual jugs, and, instead of bread, guests are presented with plates of *matzah*, the unleavened bread that Jews have been devouring at Passover each year for centuries – but which here, in homage to a community all but lost, is served year-round.

Outside, a light rain begins to fall. In the grey of a Kraków spring day, suddenly the air is melancholy and bittersweet. In a country to which it had seemed lost, Jewish life is being recreated. But it is another Jewish life. And the other world that once flourished here has all but gone – even as its last survivors still breathe.

Acknowledgements

Many people have contributed in countless ways to this book. I thank all those who suggested survivors, those who assisted with research in Australia and Poland – especially Avril Alba, Sue Hampel, Konrad Kwiet, and Renee Symonds – and the families and friends of interviewees.

My endless gratitude goes to this book's eighteen survivors for so generously recalling such a terrible period of their lives and its ramifications. Spending time with you has been one of the highlights of a long and rewarding career. You have made me laugh and cry, and above all think. Thank you for all those conversations. You have forever enriched my life.

I am grateful, too, for the few but unforgettable encounters I had with the late Magda Singer. A survivor with an untold story, she was the inspiration for this book.